# LEST WE FORGET

A Personal Reflection on the Formation of
The Orthodox Presbyterian Church

## Robert King Churchill

The Committee for the Historian
of
The Orthodox Presbyterian Church

ISBN 0-934688-34-6

To Our Children
and Their Children

A LEGACY

"But we have this treasure in jars of clay
to show that this all-surpassing power is
from God and not from us."

2 Corinthians 4:7

Robert K. Churchill
(1960)

# TABLE OF CONTENTS

# PREFACE

I first met the Rev. Robert K. Churchill nearly thirty years ago while he was pastor of Calvary Orthodox Presbyterian Church in Cedar Grove, Wisconsin. I had recently graduated from Westminster Theological Seminary and had received a call to pastor First Orthodox Presbyterian Church of Waterloo, Iowa. We met at the presbytery meeting where I was to be examined for licensure and eventual ordination.

Mr. Churchill was a big man in all respects, and I soon determined that I would not knowingly cross this man if I could help it! My initial impression of this gifted man was softened, however, when I attended my first youth camp at Camp Calvin. Mr. Churchill was there and his leadership was prominent and unique. In various ways, including a special creative-writing class which he taught, he challenged the young people to exercise their gifts and develop a greater awareness of God's marvelous creation. My appreciation for Mr. Churchill deepened as I saw a man who loved life intensely, loved young people and had a passion for the great doctrines of the faith I had come to embrace at Westminster Seminary.

About a year after I met Mr. Churchill, he and the late Rev. John Verhage (then pastor of Bethel Orthodox Presbyterian Church in Oostburg, Wisconsin) came as a visitation committee of the presbytery to the Waterloo church I was serving. Their arrival was providentially timed. There were no crises in the church but one had developed in my own life and ministry. These mature servants of the Lord ministered to me, a floundering young pastor, and that day they offered me the kind of encouragement so often needed by young men just beginning their ministries. After their departure, I thanked God for these two fathers in the faith who gave me the sound counsel from the word of God that enabled me to persevere.

The Rev. and Mrs. Churchill eventually left Wisconsin for home-mission work in California. After that our contacts were infrequent until my pastorates were interrupted in 1974 by a stint as general secretary of our denominational Committee on Home Missions and Church Extension. By this time Mr. Churchill's ministry had focused on pioneer church-planting ventures in New Mexico and Texas. Our common labor in home missions caused our correspondence to become more regular and our paths to cross more and more frequently. I also had the privilege of preaching at his installation service as organizing pastor in Roswell, New Mexico. During those days, the twenty-eight-year gap in our ages began to narrow, and the father-to-son relationship I had enjoyed became more of a brother-to-brother relationship. I even began to call him Bob! As we were able to correspond and discuss various church concerns, my appreciation of his insights concerning the trends of our day began to grow. He gleaned many of these insights, I discovered, from his wide experience in the early days of his ministry.

Several days prior to his death we had breakfast together at a presbytery meeting in the Chicago area. We discussed matters pertaining to Westminster Theological Seminary in Philadelphia, where we were both serving on the Board of Trustees. During that conversation he mentioned that he was still working on a history of The Orthodox Presbyterian Church. This was good news, since I was convinced that Bob would be able to write that history as no one else in the denomination could. I encouraged him in this task and looked forward to the day when I could read the manuscript. I certainly did not realize then that I would be the one to complete the task. But God's ways are not always ours.

On God's calendar the day arrived for Bob to lay down his pen for the last time. The date — Saturday September 20, 1980. Though semiretired, he was preparing to preach the next day at Falls Orthodox Presbyterian Church in Menomonee Falls, Wisconsin when he was stricken by a fatal heart attack.

Soon after his death, a number of his acquaintances who knew of his writing project on the history of The Orthodox Presbyterian Church encouraged his wife Dorothy to pursue publication of the book. However, once the material written by her husband was examined, it became obvious that his other pursuits of preaching, teaching and correspondence had taken precedence over this endeavor: the manuscript was still in outline and rough-draft form.

Nonetheless, after Dorothy lovingly and painstakingly searched through his accumulated writings, an unfinished yet insightful history of The Orthodox Presbyterian Church began to emerge. I subsequently agreed to assist in editing the material for possible publication. The task was formidable. I quickly discovered that Bob had actually been working on two writing projects; one was the history of the denomination and the other an autobiography. These projects were distinct, but there was also a great deal of overlap. It became my task to take these strands and weave them together into a single book.

I was assisted in this work by the labor of many hands. Two members of the church I was serving (Grace Orthodox Presbyterian Church in Vienna, Virginia), Bill and Joyce Brogden, encouraged me in this endeavor and also spent considerable hours in putting the first edited version on computer disks. Joyce's expertise as an English teacher provided invaluable assistance in preparing the rough drafts.

Copies of the draft were sent to several people, including the Rev. and Mrs. Lewis Grotenhuis, who offered many helpful suggestions. The Rev. Douglas Felch and his wife Susan also read the manuscript and soon were brought into the project in view of their writing and editing skills. I am deeply indebted to Doug for the many hours he spent editing the book and preparing the final draft for publication.

I have also been assisted and encouraged throughout this endeavor by Dorothy Churchill, who experienced firsthand most of the history recounted in the pages that follow. She was the author's constant companion throughout the forty-seven years of their married life. Our correspondence regarding the manuscript gave me keen insight into the character of this godly woman, whose support of her husband's ministry undoubtedly caused him to rise up and call her blessed.

My previous contacts with Dorothy had been as a guest in their home, where her gifts of hospitality were evident. But our work together on this project has enabled me to appreciate some of her many other talents. She is a woman of the Word who shares her late husband's love for the truth once for all delivered to the saints. Though now an octogenarian, she is still vitally interested in the ongoing history of the church in which she and her husband served so faithfully.

As the book began to take final form, the matter of financing its publication presented another challenge. I am grateful to the Committee on Christian Education of The Orthodox Presbyterian Church for its decision to endorse the project, and to the numerous individuals who contributed financially to make possible its publication.

When we first began to work on this project, the semicentennial of The Orthodox Presbyterian Church was several years away; but the amount of time involved in organizing and editing the manuscript for publication has brought us close to this 50th anniversary year—1986. Although not part of the original plan, it is fitting that this historical account be published on the occasion of our observance of a significant milestone in the life of The Orthodox Presbyterian Church. This book is especially important for those who do not know of Dr. J. Gresham Machen, a godly scholar and churchman whose life was entwined with the events leading up to the formation of The Orthodox Presbyterian Church. It is our hope that those who read these pages will benefit from the insights of Mr. Churchill. His gifts of analyzing and reflecting upon the events recorded here can better equip the present generation to meet the challenges of our day.

GEORGE E. HANEY

Vienna, Virginia
September 1985

# 1

## *BETHEL REVISITED*

I push open the great studded doors and step across the threshold into yesterday. Thirty years have rolled by. Memories of happy days gone by well up within me, all fresh and green.

I have just stepped into the old First Presbyterian Church in Tacoma, Washington at 10th and G Streets. The auditorium is much the same as it used to be. I wish I could express what I feel as I stand here all alone in the silence. The light of a garish day is diffused through beautiful stained-glass windows. As I sit here in the back pew under the balcony, the memories come flooding back.

It was in this old church, with its red carpet and dark-stained woodwork, that I first heard the gospel. It was in this church that I first came to love the songs of Zion. I was converted and baptized in this church. I first met my wife here. It was also here that I was called into the gospel ministry.

I remember the friend who originally brought me to the church and the first time I climbed those stairs to the balcony where the young men's class met. I recall how uncomfortable I felt when I was first handed a Bible. The discomfort turned to panic, however, when the teacher asked the class to turn to the book of Daniel. I didn't know where the book was located, what it was about, or even who Daniel was! I will always be grateful to the young man who so easily and completely ended my panic by leaning over and handing me a Bible opened to the right place.

After Sunday School my friend and I went downstairs for the morning worship service. We sat to the right of the center aisle. On that day, at eighteen years of age, I first heard the gospel preached. I can still remember the text, though not the sermon. I was soon to learn that then, as now, the text was more important than the sermon.

I can still remember Dr. C. W. Weyer striding into the pulpit. The congregation listened and responded to his preaching, which was strong and vigorous. He had a prose style and the spirit of an artist. The message was prophetic and warned of the rising apostasy called modernism. The strength of his exegesis was commanding. He knew he was expounding the word of God. The truth was clear-cut and he felt a burden to inspire souls to hunger for Christ.

Memories! How impressed I was that morning at the singing of one of the hymns, most of them new to me, of course. I will never forget the words the woman behind me was singing —

14

Awake, my soul in joyful lays,
And sing thy great Redeemer's praise;
He justly claims a song from me,
His loving-kindness is so free.

That woman was a young wife and mother who has since left the earthly congregation and now sings a nobler, sweeter song in heaven.

I think also of Mr. Omar Berry, who could sing the gospel message as no one else I have ever heard. His mortal voice, too, is now still. But through eyes a little misty I can yet see his face and hear his baritone voice ringing out —

The sands have been washed in the footprints
Of the stranger on Galilee's shore —
And the voice that subdued the rough billows
Will be heard in Judea no more.

Mr. Berry would often sing a solo after the Sunday evening sermon. I can still picture his swarthy features. He would throw his head back in abandon, not with the style or sophistication of a Hollywood star, but with a power unmatched by any singer of that day. And Oh, that simple singing, sometimes reaching the rafters and sometimes reduced to a whisper — every word could be heard. A gentle stillness would come over the congregation as Omar's melodious voice filled every corner of the building. God spoke to my dead soul more than once through that singing —

God calling yet; shall I not hear?
Earth's pleasures shall I still hold dear?
Shall earth's swift passing years all fly
And still my soul in slumber lie?

15

This music, following strong preaching, and in the atmosphere of faith and prayer, was an instrument of the Holy Spirit that stirred my soul. For here, in this old-style auditorium with its high, domed ceiling, I began to see the light and at the same time to wrestle with the Prince of Darkness. Here it was I first heard Christ's sweet voice calling, here that I first knew the drawing power of the cross and felt myself yielding. Here, under sound doctrinal preaching, the pillars of a mighty plan appeared — built by the architect that built the sky.

I, however, fought hard against God's workings in my life. I had more pride than most, and doubts often overwhelmed me. But it was in this setting that the irresistible grace of God sought and found me. Just now, the intervening years seem to have dissolved, and I am alone with him who first called my name and beckoned me.

In those days of inner struggle it helped a great deal to meet others who were going through a similar experience. In young peoples' meetings, but especially in the midweek prayer meetings that I and others my age attended, I often heard testimonies that were an encouragement to me. The church was evangelical in a fervent, yet not unnatural, way. The evangelical spirit and outreach were undergirded by constant Bible study. In this auditorium which seated six or seven hundred people I heard many well-known evangelists who were the great Bible teachers of the day. The church held special meetings lasting two or three weeks at least once a year. The minister tried to invite, as he put it, "the best preachers in the world." Hearing these men speak was an education in itself.

I remember well hearing G. Campbell Morgan preach. What an impression he made in the city of Tacoma! Both his appearance and manner of address were striking. Yet what especially impressed his listeners was his subject matter. He related the stories of the Bible extremely well. I heard an attorney say in a bewildered tone, "All Dr. Morgan did was stand there and give the outline of a Bible book, yet what rapt attention fell on the crowd." Let none suppose that this outlining of the contents of a chapter or book of the Bible was done without training. Behind what appeared to be effortless preaching was clearly a lifetime of discipline and study.

As I continue to sit and reminisce in this old church building, more memories flood my mind. I can see just ahead of me, on the left side of the aisle, the pew where I first sat beside a certain girl named Dorothy, who later became my wife. We had been working together with a group that often went to the gospel mission downtown on Saturday nights. Dorothy had a unique voice. It was not in the least theatrical but it communicated her message very well. One night I heard her sing a message that went straight to my sinful heart—

Are you too heavy-laden?
Come, sinner, come!
Jesus will bear your burden,
Come, sinner, come!

She was singing the gospel to the needy assembled in the mission on Pacific Avenue, but her song made me feel that I was the biggest sinner there. Today this same girl is typing this manuscript for me.

It was in this church, as well, that the Lord called me to the gospel ministry. The assistant pastor of our Tacoma church was a young man who had not yet been to seminary, but in whose face and person the Holy Spirit shone. Christ was real to him. Christ was his only message. I remember one of the nights he led the midweek prayer meeting and Bible study in the pastor's absence. The word of God was precious to us that night and the glory of God came down. I cannot now recall just what the lesson was, but I can still remember the stirrings of my soul.

Have you ever felt the presence of the Holy Spirit upon hearing the word? Well, that night he came rushing, welling up within me after the meeting — wave upon wave, surge upon surge — what unspeakable joy!

I walked home that night experiencing a great fullness. At the house I tried to read, tried to forget, but it was no use. God was calling. I got up and went out on the porch high above the street overlooking the city.

What did I do then? I did something very human and probably quite sinful. I prayed compulsively, "Please don't overpower me so, Lord — I can't stand it." Such wonder and joy, such overwhelming love was beyond my human comprehension. Deep was calling unto deep and I was caught in that most marvelous undertow.

So it was that here in this old church structure the Holy Spirit came to me, a common sinner. He came to me through the word, embraced me and called me into the ministry. In my own mind I was by no means ready when I first heard that unmistakable call. I had not yet even made a public profession of faith and become a member of the church. Indeed, I think one reason I delayed so long was because I feared the Lord might want me to be a preacher, and I certainly had no ability or education for that. I was nearly twenty years old and had not even finished grade school!

It was not too long after this that I became engaged to the girl of the lovely voice. Perhaps subconsciously, I thought that one way to frustrate the leadings and promotings of the Holy Spirit in regard to a call to the ministry would be to marry the woman.

How foolish to fight and plan against God! Everything was ready for our wedding. The date was set, the wedding dress was all made, and the ring had been engraved. But as it turned out, the wedding was postponed for seven years while I went to school. I attempted a short cut, via a course in the Bible Institute of Los Angeles. But "No," said that inner voice, "get a thorough education, the best available, before you preach the word." So, through common sense and by his grace, I learned the lesson often written in tears and agony: "My utmost for his highest." Surely God leads us, and not by any shortcuts either!

Nonetheless, no man can ever take the slightest credit for becoming a minister. I became a minister because I had to. As it came to Paul, so in a lesser way it came to me: "Yea, woe is me if I preach not the gospel!"

So now I am here again at my Bethel, my House of God, where love and mercy found me.

But enough of nostalgia. The currents of life have moved rapidly and significantly in the last century. In the twenties and thirties First Presbyterian Church of Tacoma, and others of its kind, stood at the crossroads of mighty upheavals in the religious life of America. From the events that subsequently took place we may find both inspiration and warning, for there were weaknesses in the Tacoma church. These weaknesses were not, at the time of my conversion, fully developed, but more like subtle tendencies or small doctrinal oversights. Somehow certain doctrines of an unpresbyterian and unscriptural nature were allowed entrance into that church. The result is history — a history the lessons of which, I trust, will benefit the modern-day reader.

In the chapters that follow I wish to trace the history of First Church and other churches up to our own day. It may be heartbreaking and a bit bewildering to some. But I think the reader will come to see that a knowledge of the past is essential for a right understanding of the religious and moral currents of our day.

# 2

## GIANTS

In the previous chapter, *Bethel Revisited,* I attempted to relate briefly the story of my conversion and call to the ministry in the old First Presbyterian Church of Tacoma, Washington. First Presbyterian Church was one of the great churches of its day. But what happened to it? Let us look at that church, both concerning its subsequent history and also the picture it gives us of the present state of Christendom.

The church that grew up with Tacoma stood for something special on that hillside overlooking the young city. Pastor and congregation took a courageous and outspoken stand against the modernism and unbelief that were at that time striving for supremacy in national and church life. There were many sermons warning about the course that the denomination, the then Presbyterian Church in the United States of America, seemed to be taking. Sermons preached after each general assembly were especially earnest. We were made to see the great gulf that separated so-called liberal theology from the historic Christian faith.

Dr. Weyer, the pastor, was a strong man; there was no compromise in his nature. He raised a strong and fearless voice in defense of the word of God. There were those who resented this. As a result, he was sometimes ridiculed, hated and reviled, particularly by some of the wealthier church members. They would dismiss the issue by saying, "Savanarola preached this morning." (Savanarola was a famous Italian preacher of the fifteenth century whose sermons were characterized by a strong denunciation of current sins and calls for repentance.) Despite such opposition, Dr. Weyer commanded a hearing and raised the standard high.

Let me cite some of the more sterling qualities that were prevalent in the Tacoma church, for surely they are worthy of emulation. The Tacoma church was blessed with strong leadership. "There is always something doing in that pulpit," wrote a visiting reporter. The pastor preached the word of God and therein lay the church's strength. The text always stood out.

Another factor that made the church grow and gave it spirit was the pastor's boldness in speaking out on many issues of civic and national interest. He was aware of what was going on in the world. He was a preacher of the word who met the times. This was very far from the so-called social gospel of the liberal, or the fads-of-the-day preacher so often encountered. Weyer could see world movements in the light of the word of God. He often preached on prophecy, but the audience was not lost in a maze of needless, detailed interpretations. Rather, there was breadth and scope to his preaching along with a strong reliance on common sense.

The spirit of evangelism was very strong in the Tacoma church. I have never seen a church more active. Its people were great inviters. In a thousand ways the whole church was reaching out. The members of the young men's class that I first attended were out on the streets visiting people each week.

I remember, even before I attended the church, seeing a great footprint stamped in indelible ink on many sidewalk corners in Tacoma. This huge footprint was pointed in the general direction of First Church, and inside were stamped these words: "Hear Weyer — First Presby. Church." This was the work of the men in the men's Sunday-night club, a large group organized with one purpose only — to fill the church to capacity every Sunday night. I firmly believe that every church ought to have such a club. Certainly Sunday nights were great occasions in that church!

Seattle was a kind of twin city to Tacoma and one that held a lot of fascination for me. I write now of a church and its ministry in that city because it helps expand upon the theme of this book. One of the more colorful ministers there was Dr. Mark A. Matthews. His ministry in First Presbyterian Church covered a period of almost forty years. I am much indebted to the ministry of that church, for I was strengthened by worshiping there while a student at the University of Washington in Seattle.

Dr. Matthews was a striking figure. Because of his height (about six feet, six inches) he was often called "The Tall Pine of the Sierras." In the pulpit he wore a Prince Albert coat and seldom stood behind a pulpit desk while preaching. He would stand or walk about in utter freedom. Without notes and with great power he proclaimed the gospel. He came to Seattle from the

South on the specified condition that the church would be the minister's *force* and not his *field*. Dr. Matthews never went to college or seminary but received his theological training by the old method of sitting at the feet of an older minister. He had evidently heard great preaching and had been expertly trained by this method.

Dr. Matthews was by no means pulpit-bound. He often carried the torch of civic righteousness. More than once he marched his parishioners down to the courthouse to demand a change in the corrupt police department. Occasionally a newcomer would be startled to learn that, under his Prince Albert, Dr. Matthews wore the badge of a deputy sheriff!

He also had embraced a rugged Calvinistic theology. For thirty-eight years he stood and made his voice heard. He gathered around him a church of eight thousand members and twenty-seven branch Sunday Schools. It was often remarked that "Matthews made Seattle presbyterian."

The influence of Dr. Matthews, however it may be evaluated, was not exercised through the use of soft words or by soft-pedaling the more difficult doctrines of the faith. In university circles, his church was often called "the cattle barn." But I noticed that many came from the more liberal churches to hear him preach.

Many were the stories told of the exploits of this prophet of the Lord when he was in his prime. I had a friend in the university who was working on his advanced degree. He and his mother had been members of Dr. Matthews's congregation. This friend was no longer sympathetic to his preaching, but he nevertheless told the story of how Dr. Matthews had once preached in crowded auditoriums the "awesome" doctrines of Calvinism. Sometimes, at the close of a particularly strong and impressive sermon, the congregation would sit for several minutes as if stunned. On one such occasion my friend said to his mother, "Mother, what's the matter with the people?"

Dr. Matthews was the speaker at a sunrise service one Easter morning. I was not present, but I heard the report made by some young ladies from the university circle. They came back infuriated. They said that thousands and thousands of people had been gathered together at the service. The park in the early morning was so beautiful, and in such surroundings the people were full of hope and aspiration. One felt uplifted by the very sight. But what did Dr. Matthews do? "He preached on the flames of hell, and then proved to us from the Bible," the girls said, "that we were all going there! Imagine a minister acting like that, especially on such an occasion! He missed a golden opportunity and spoiled the day for thousands."

Dr. Matthews's strength was declining when I came under his ministry. Nevertheless he could still virtually shake the place. His preaching did something to people — he possessed and stirred men. He communicated his ideas well, but that was not his main purpose. He was not preaching doctrine for doctrine's sake—he was after the hearts of men. And he usually got what he was after.

Part of Dr. Matthews's power as a preacher lay in his sense of drama. One Sunday morning I heard him preach on the subject of prayer. During the message he was emphasizing the point that true prayer must come from a born-again person, one who is a child of God through faith in Jesus Christ. To illustrate this point, he stepped back and sat in his pulpit chair. Since there was no pulpit desk in front, all could easily see him. He told about (and acted the part of) an important businessman sitting at his desk; there were important papers, telephones and an intercom before him. Around him were secretaries, clerks, and people demanding attention. What a busy scene! And then it happened. The door suddenly opened and in came his young son.

"Father," he cried — and immediately that busy man looked at his little boy and said, "Come here, son, and tell me what you want." By this time the minister was sitting in his large chair with his legs crossed, totally relaxed, having a homey chat with his child. Matthews then made a sweeping gesture with his long arm, brushing all imaginary business from his desk. "This little boy is the main business now," he said. "Father and son are in a relationship that rises above all others in importance."

"Are you a child of God by being born again?" Matthews continued. "Can you pray, 'Our Father who art in heaven'? If so, your Father will hear you." The illustration had taken but a few minutes. But for those who heard it, the story would not soon be forgotten.

Dr. Matthews, as I have previously noted, had no formal education in theology. A careful observer could detect this, especially in his later years. But how that man could preach! I wonder if that kind of preaching exists today. I have not heard such preaching by men who have spent long years in seminary and who have earned advanced degrees. I do not mean to disparage education. I have seen far too much ignorance and lack of adequate training in the ministry to do that. My point is simply this: it takes an extraordinary man to finish an adequate education and still be a John the Baptist.

Looking back and reflecting on the men behind the pulpits in Seattle and Tacoma, it is marvelous to remember how God worked in their lives. The natural forcefulness of men like Matthews and Weyer was awesome in itself, and their deliveries were powerful. But over the years I have observed that there are times in all great preaching when a supernatural power prevails — the power of the Holy Spirit. At those times the natural force of a man is kept in check, and a higher power is unleashed. The sermon flows, and the doctrine distills as the dew from heaven. Thus was the preaching in those golden days of strength and unity.

When Dr. Matthews returned from a general assembly, even back in the twenties, Seattle knew what to expect. The great church would be packed on the following Sunday. In his precise, dramatic manner Dr. Matthews would outline the ways in which the modernistic machine was working to push its doctrines and policies. How well he knew them! He had a fine mind as well as a fighting spirit. Then with true prophetic insight he would predict the triumph of unbelief in the Presbyterian Church in the United States of America and the division that would eventually take place between the forces of Christ and the forces of the Antichrist. As a climax, and with great power, Dr. Matthews would declare that he would be the first to lead out the armies of the Lord from a corrupt denomination.

Needless to say, the congregation was with him almost to a man. Here was a daring Moses, challenging the might of a Pharaoh. History would come alive at these times, and the people were to be a vital part of it.

I wish — how I wish — that this section of the story could have a more triumphant ending. I would spare you the sad anticlimax if I could. It reminds me of

T. S. Eliot's saying that the world, or history, does not end with a bang but with a whimper.

I write of the churches in Seattle and Tacoma to help illustrate the happenings in other places. In later years the kind of fearless exegesis described above degenerated. It was then that the notes in the *Scofield Reference Bible* became more and more prominent in the preaching in both the Seattle and Tacoma churches. These notes, and the interpretation of Scripture upon which they were based, were contrary to our presbyterian and Reformed heritage. This shift in thinking would have dire consequences in later years.

# 3

## *A HERITAGE LOST*

I am .now faced with an unpleasant task. Having touched on some of their strengths, I must now write of the weaknesses in the Tacoma and Seattle churches. I wish to make an important observation. Drs. Weyer and Matthews were fearless fundamentalists. They stood firm for the faith once delivered unto the saints. But what these men and others like them did not seem to realize was that a new kind of fundamentalism was quickly growing up around them — one quite different from what they and their fathers had preached. There were still giants in the earth in those days, but the giants allowed their children to feed upon that which could never nourish a race of giants!

In the twenties and thirties these pastors — and others like them — stood with their congregations at the crossroads. The religious ferment taking place in America at this very critical time was introducing certain doctrines of an un-Reformed and unscriptural nature into the church. Unless we see plainly this shift of theological and spiritual winds, we will fail to understand why the conservatives in the Presbyterian Church were later unable to maintain a united testimony against the forces of modernism. We will also be utterly confused by the different usage of the same terminology.

Let me explain for a moment what I mean. Historically, the term *fundamentalist* refers to those people who, in contrast to the theological liberals (or modernists) upheld what came to be known as the Five Fundamentals of the faith. These were: (1) the inspiration and infallibility of the Scriptures; (2) the virgin birth of Christ; (3) the miracles of Christ; (4) the substitutionary atonement of Christ; and (5) belief in the bodily resurrection of Christ. These are beliefs essential to historic Christianity. Therefore every true Christian who upholds these truths is a fundamentalist.

Since every Calvinist or Reformed believer also upholds these essential doctrines of the Christian faith, they may consider themselves fundamentalists in the truest sense of the term. However, adherents to the Reformed faith would argue that there are more doctrines essential to the Christian faith than merely the five mentioned above. In other words, they believe in more fundamentals than the fundamentalists do. But here is the irony of the situation — much of modern fundamentalism, which upholds these five fundamentals, attacks many of the other important fundamentals of the faith which Reformed people have always cherished and have shed their blood to maintain.

Parenthetically, it should be said that unless we are willing to face these facts squarely, we simply cannot understand the struggle and disappointments that later came to Dr. J. Gresham Machen, to Westminster Seminary and to The Orthodox Presbyterian Church. The split in that church only a few years after it began and the formation of the Bible Presbyterian Synod can only be understood in a larger context — a context in which one branch of fundamentalism (and a very powerful one at that) departed from the mainstream of historic and biblical Christianity and the fullness of the Reformed faith. How and why this unfortunate development took place is the subject of this chapter.

Sometime before I attended the Tacoma church, Dr. Lewis Sperry Chafer delivered a series of lectures on the subject of grace. (The same material now appears in his book entitled *Grace.*) On the surface it seemed to be a new emphasis on the grace of God and a restatement of the grand Pauline doctrine of salvation by grace apart from the deeds of the law. But alas, how opposed it was to Paul's views, both of law and of grace. This book should not, however, be entirely condemned, for there is much good in it. The subject of God's grace is surprisingly rich, even when insufficiently treated. Even so, there is no question of the inadequacy of Chafer's treatment of the relationship of law and grace.

Dr. Machen, founder of Westminster Theological Seminary and professor of New Testament, used to remind us that "a right view of the law makes man a seeker after grace," and also, "We are not saved by the law, but we are saved unto the law." These two phrases summarize the proper dual role of the law in God's work of salvation. First, man realizes how desperately he needs grace only when he comes face to face with the holiness of God reflected in the law. Only then will he realize the hopelessness of trying to be justified before God on the basis of obedience to the law. Second, we are saved by grace apart from the works of the law. But the purpose of grace is holiness, not lawlessness. After God has saved a man, the law teaches him how to live a life of gratitude to God for so great a deliverance. In this way the law of God is essential for understanding both man's need for grace and man's proper response to grace.

But Chafer's treatment of the subject of grace never arrives at the right view of the law of God. According to Dr. Chafer, the law was a condition of salvation placed upon the people of God in the Old Testament during a special and limited time period — the Dispensation of Law. This condition, Chafer contended, no longer has application to the New Testament believer since we relate to God under a new dispensation, the Dispensation of Grace. Since, as he put it, "we are no longer under law, but under grace," Chafer argued that there is no necessary relationship between law and grace. Here is law without grace, and grace without law. Always and in every sense, law and grace are opposed to each other.

This teaching appears to be scriptural, but in reality it was the ancient error of antinomianism (antilaw) which denies that the law has application to the Christian. Chafer defended this view by means of a radical reinterpretation of the Scriptures. The Bible was divided into several separate time periods, or dispensations, during which mankind was tested in respect to obedience to some specific revelation of the will of God. While running the risk of oversimplifying Chafer's position, we must recognize that the practical consequence of adopting his viewpoint is to believe that God dealt with mankind and offered the promise of salvation in different ways in differing periods of redemptive history. That is why Chafer can argue that law has nothing to do with grace. This view, known as dispensationalism, was originally put forth in the nineteenth century by John Nelson Darby and popularized and widely disseminated by the study notes of the *Scofield Reference Bible.* It was this religion without law, or opposed to law, that would increasingly characterize the new fundamentalism. It also constituted the vortex into which modern evangelicalism would be drawn.

More important for our purposes, dispensationalism was also a frontal attack on covenant theology and the doctrine of the unity of the covenant of grace held since the time of the Reformation. These truths were also clearly taught in the secondary standards of American Presbyterianism, the Westminster Confession of Faith and the larger and shorter catechisms. The doctrine of the unity of the covenant of grace teaches that the people of God in both the New Testament and the Old Testament are saved by God's grace, not on the basis of their good works. It also argues for the essential unity of the Old Testament and New Testament people of God. Both of these truths are obscured in dispensationalism.

For example, in the dispensational scheme of instruction, the New Testament church is viewed as a parenthesis in the history of redemption — a time-out period when God's great prophetic clock stopped ticking. That is, the church is only a temporary development in God's plan to which the Lord has committed the gospel, until the kingdom is once again restored to the nation of Israel. The dispensationalist defends this idea on the basis of a literal interpretation of certain Old Testament promises. I used to teach this myself. But later I began to wonder how it was that the church, which was the mystical body of Christ and the pillar and ground of the truth, could be so unforeseen and inconsequential.

Likewise, those of us who taught dispensationalism stirred up a pious excitement by pointing out that the Jews, God's chosen people, were returning to Jerusalem. This meant, we believed, that prophecy was being fulfilled before our very eyes. Not once did we remember Paul's words, "A man is not a Jew if he is only one outwardly" (Rom. 2:28), or recall that believers in Christ were the true children of Abraham (Gal. 3:29). Neither did we realize that no prophecy could be fulfilled outside of Christ.

To this day I am ashamed of the way my colleagues and I misused Scripture to try to support such notions. There is not a shred of scriptural evidence for them. How simple, yet how revolutionary, is the teaching of Scripture that there is only one people of God in all ages. There is only one chosen people, chosen in Christ before the world began (Eph. 1:3-6). This is not to say that there are no differences between the church in the Old Testament and the church in the New Testament. For example, the church in the Old Testament was mainly national, while the church in the New Testament is international. But such differences should not obscure the similarities between the Old Testament and the New Testament people of God. We have the same Savior, the same salvation, the same God. The true Israel was the church of the Old Testament, and the true church is the Israel of the New Testament. While this is glorious truth to those holding to the unity, or wholeness, of the word of God, it is almost heresy to the dispensationalist.

If one is acquainted with both the Reformed faith and the teachings and implications of dispensationalism, he will clearly see that the two approaches are diametrically opposed to each other at many points. For the most part these differences are the very same ones that exist today between the Reformed faith and modern fundamentalism. Some may think these differences are nonessential, but we view them as absolutely critical. Each has a different view of the grace of God, of the law of God, of the church of God, of the word of God and of the salvation of God. There is revealed in each a different way of going about living the Christian life, a different approach to worship, of preaching the truth and of evaluating events both secular and ecclesiastical. In fact, the dispensationalist has practically reduced the broad range of Christian responsibility to two obligations: save souls and preach the second coming. It is true that champions of certain fundamental doctrines have come forth from among the dispensationalists, but often these champions know or care nothing for the glorious scope of the whole counsel of God that has characterized our Reformation heritage.

The fact that such teachings were welcomed in the Tacoma church seems strange. The serious errors in the lectures of Dr. Chafer apparently were not detected or, if they were, they were not considered serious. Therefore, it was not long before these aberrations began to seep into the teaching of the church.

I can still remember when the *Scofield Bible Correspondence Course* from Moody Bible Institute in Chicago was first introduced into First Presbyterian Church's Sunday School. I was one of several who took that three-year course. We used three large books on theology and would send our examinations to the institute to be corrected. A new class was organized every six to twelve months. Later, several classes were in progress at once. These courses became more or less teacher-training courses for the church.

The use of the Scofield Bible course had many positive results, but it also led the church in a certain direction that was most significant in light of the life-and-death struggle that would soon descend upon the church. The church was steered away from its high Calvinistic standards and toward the direction of dispensationalism, antinomianism and Arminianism. The church was not destroyed, but the strength of its theology was diminished.

We who were taking the Scofield course used to enjoy sharing our "insights" during another class or meeting. Sometimes we would set forth the view that there were many gospels, or that the law was only for the Jews, or that the church was not in the Old Testament. The pastor of the Tacoma church did not always agree with these doctrines, and it would not take him long to set us straight.

I remember visiting a special class of young men who were planning to enter the ministry. This group met prior to the midweek prayer meeting and was taught by Dr. Matthews. On this occasion, some of those earnest young men were voicing certain popular dispensational views about God's law. Some even said that the moral law had been abrogated. Others held that it was bad to preach the law, or that the law stirred up evil. It was like a sign in an orchard saying, "Don't pick cherries," because it created the desire to sin. What did Dr. Matthews say about this?

I shall never forget the forcefulness and clarity with which he boldly set forth both the awful majesty and all-embracing authority of the law of God and the heinous character of sin. "Man can't manufacture sin," he said. "The law which sin violates is the law of God." This answer, I later discovered, was good Reformed theology.

How then, you may ask, could such strong churches welcome into their teaching ministry a course like the Scofield Bible course—and with it Darby dispensationalism? Couldn't the church leaders recognize such un-Reformed and unscriptural instruction? The answer is not a simple one, but this at least can be said: fundamentalism in its non-Calvinistic form came into the Presbyterian Church to fill a vacuum. This vacuum existed because the church was no longer teaching the Confession of Faith and catechisms in any adequate or vital way.

I am grateful that in the Tacoma church, as in many others, the gospel was being proclaimed; but much was also missing. Neither in the sermons nor in Bible classes or discussion groups did members become acquainted with the Westminster Confession of Faith or the larger and shorter catechisms. Nor did I ever hear a sermon or lesson on the Ten Commandments. Infant baptism was administered but the pastor never explained its underlying covenant theology, nor did he teach why the sacrament itself was administered. Thus, we had no answers to give in response either to the scoffing or to the sincere questions of our Baptist brothers. "Easygesis" (easy exegesis) of Scripture was often substituted for more scholarly exegesis and this allowed portions of Scripture, often taken out of context, to be forced into a human scheme of prophecy.

Since many of the mistaken doctrines of dispensationalism were constantly being taught in the church, and since there was often no obvious clash, the minister did not always take the time to correct the situation.

After all, it was a Bible study, and people seemed to be growing spiritually from it. It seemed that the pastor of such a large church was occupied with "bigger things." The minister was too busy to investigate such things as materials for Sunday School and the kind of instruction being given to the young people.

This situation in the Tacoma and Seattle churches was being repeated in hundreds of other Presbyterian churches at the time. I am not referring to those churches that had gone over to the modernistic or liberal camp. Rather, I refer to those churches that were bravely standing for the fundamentals of the faith — those who believed the Scriptures to be the word of God. In many such churches the vacuum created by failure to preserve their Reformed heritage was being filled by dispensationalism, thus weakening the church. The timing of this development couldn't have been more unfortunate. The Bible-believing churches were being ostracized and attacked. The chill winds of modernism and secularism were keenly felt. Something had to be found to rekindle the fires of devotion and strengthen the people of God. There was also a need for weapons to use in the deadly warfare that was gradually engulfing the church.

While help was desperately needed, it was difficult for the churches to know where to find it. Naturally the first suggestion would be to go to the boards and agencies of the denomination. Many tried, but to their dismay and confusion they found the agencies of the church themselves honeycombed with unbelief. There was no help there at all. The Presbyterian schools and seminaries had also succumbed. The enervating effects of modernism and unbelief had seemingly prevailed.

In desperation, the Bible-believing churches had to turn somewhere. Where did they turn? The answer is most significant. In that desperate hour they turned quite naturally to the independent Bible institutes. Here were institutions that still held to the word of God. And thank God for that! Unfortunately, most of these institutions were dispensational in their perspective. Dr. Chafer became president of Dallas Theological Seminary which, in turn, was a major training center of the evangelical and Bible-believing churches in the days when the crucial battles between modernism and historical Christianity were shaping up. And so it was, in that desperate hour, the Bible-believing churches turned to Dallas Seminary, Bible institutes and various other sincere Bible-believing, though un-Reformed, institutions.

The full import of this was not seen until years later. The churches that had been reborn and nurtured in the revival of the scriptural teaching of Calvin and the Reformation turned in a new but certain direction. The student of contemporary church history, as well as anyone who wishes to understand the modern age, would do well to ponder this direction and this shift.

Calvinism in the past had kept back the tides of Romanism and unbelief. Those who believed in the sovereignty of God were in the forefront of every battle for true freedom. They were the force in the whole of society. But where is that force today? The ancient enemies of the church are having a field day. They are not even being challenged. Why is there no real antidote in Protestantism today for the poisons of Romanism and modernism? There was at one time.

I am persuaded that a large part of the answer is to be found in the direction the believing church was forced to turn during those most fateful years. There is a difference between Calvinism and modern fundamentalism, and this difference has resulted in tragic consequences for both the church and the world. Not only has modern fundamentalism attacked some of the great and precious doctrines of the faith, but — what is more to the point in this instance — it has diminished in a very real sense the sacred deposit of truth that the Lord gave to his church. This diminished or warped theology has caused the church to lose her perspective on the real issues. It is only in this light that we can understand the contemporary scene.

The experience of First Presbyterian Church of Tacoma had a wide and prophetic significance. To a greater or lesser degree, the church life of America moved according to this pattern. The tide was turning and a glorious heritage was being lost. Modernism had enveloped the church at large, and a shallow fundamentalism was seeking to stem the flow. A more consistent and thoroughgoing return to the full teachings of the word of God had been neglected, and the consequences would soon be apparent.

Birthplace of Robert K. Churchill, Yarmouth, Nova Scotia

Bob's parents on their 50th wedding anniversary

Bob at home preparing for a Bible study before entering Biola

Bob and Dorothy on their wedding day, November 19, 1932

Graduation procession, Westminster Theological Seminary, Philadelphia, May-1939 Edwin H. Rian leads the procession, followed by Dr. McLeod, Robert Churchill, Henry Coray and John Clelland

Dorothy and Bob on graduation day

# 4

## A HERITAGE RETAINED

As described in the previous chapter, the early part of this century was marked by a general doctrinal decline in many Presbyterian churches, seminaries and Bible schools. The effects of liberalism were being felt throughout the denomination, and even churches like those in Seattle and Tacoma that successfully resisted modernist influences were retreating from their Reformed commitments and embracing dispensationalism.

In the face of these developments it is encouraging to note that there arose one institution that retained, on the one hand (over against the liberals), a strong defense of historic Christianity, and on the other (over against the dispensational fundamentalists), a staunch adherence to the full testimony of the Reformed faith. That institution was Westminster Theological Seminary in Philadelphia, Pennsylvania.

The formation of this seminary was itself a testimony to these commitments. The school was begun in 1929 to carry on the glorious tradition of old Princeton. In that year, the liberals in the Presbyterian Church in the United States of America succeeded in their attempt to reorganize Princeton Theological Seminary in order to lessen that institution's strong adherence to Reformed and historic Christianity. In response, many of the faculty and student body went across the river to Philadelphia to start the new, yet old, Westminster. From Princeton's faculty came the brilliant gifts and scholarship of men like Robert Dick Wilson, J. Gresham Machen, Oswald T. Allis and Cornelius Van Til, with John Murray following a year later.

I went to Westminster in 1933, fully aware that it was the storm center between biblical Christianity and modernism. I and the other students were not always happy to be in the center of that controversy. We could see only too clearly in the events that were rapidly unfolding that the controversy would eventually result in a tremendous struggle with far-reaching consequences.

I had not intended to go to Westminster. While attending the University of Washington in Seattle, I was registered to attend Dallas Theological Seminary. The other young men of our church were also going there. Why did I end up going to Westminster Seminary in Philadelphia instead? There were two reasons. Dr. Roy T. Brumbaugh had recently become pastor of our church in Tacoma, and he was enthusiastic about Westminster. (He later changed his mind.) But the other reason I made a switch was that I was becoming increasingly uneasy about dispensationalism.

I remember, when I was a young Christian, sitting in the midweek service in our Tacoma church. The minister had just read Isaiah 60, which begins, "Arise, shine, for your light has come, and the glory of the Lord rises upon you." Said the minister, "This is Jewish truth, not church truth." Elders and teachers present heartily agreed with the pastor. They declared that while all the Bible was *for* the church it was not all *to* the church. They spoke sadly of those misguided people who could not see the difference between Jewish truth and church truth. Kingdom truth was for the Jews. God's promise to the Jews was the promised land and worship in Jerusalem, but God's promise to the church was for salvation and heaven through Christ.

Thus were we taught in those days, and the teaching has not changed a great deal today. I remember feeling a little sad that so many strong and beautiful passages of God's word were not for the church. But I began to wonder: Could not such passages refer and apply to the church of Jesus Christ?

Along those same lines, I was frequently hearing strange things from the men at Dallas, such as: "One looks in vain for grace in the gospels." This went along with the dispensational teaching that the gospel of the kingdom, and not the gospel of grace, was in the Four Gospels. This was confusing to me, for I seemed to find very much evidence of grace in the gospels!

My uneasiness reached a critical point when I attempted to teach these ideas to others. I taught in a branch Sunday School under the supervision of First Church. I was faithfully teaching the dispensations to a group of farmers. When they began asking some innocent questions, I studied harder in order to answer them. I then realized that I was forcing the Scriptures into a plan and scheme of man's devising. At this time a catalogue of Westminster Seminary fell into my hands, and instinctively I felt firm ground under me.

Gradually, while attending Westminster, I learned the surprising yet very scriptural truth that throughout all the ages there were, and are, not two but only *one* people of God. For a prospective preacher such as I, there was no greater blessing than to be given back a whole Bible. I felt such a sense of relief and limitlessness when the departmentalizing of dispensationalism dropped away and I could revel in the whole counsel of God! I realized then that dispensationalism keeps people back from the whole heritage of the word of God.

During my first year at Westminster Seminary, I had an experience that some would call a second conversion. This "conversion," in my conscious mind at least, was accompanied by an upheaval greater than that surrounding my real conversion to Christ.

Briefly stated, this struggle brought me to a fuller understanding of, and commitment to, Calvinism. It can best be expressed by the word *largeness*. For the first time, I came to realize the greatness of the God of the Bible, and that the Bible is indeed God's self-revelation. Gradually, and in diverse ways, the doctrine of God dawned upon my soul like a cloudless morning. A reluctant assent gave way to the world-and-life view of the Reformed faith. My horizons were expanded, not by skepticism or unbelief, but by faith. I love those infinitudes that beckon the soul in the so-called Calvinistic theology. (I have used the word *so-called* advisedly. It is sad that biblical Christianity, for the sake of clarity, should have to have a man's name attached to it!)

Before I arrived at Westminster, the background of my instruction had been largely Arminian. That is, I was led to believe that it was my choice to follow God, not his decision to set his love upon me, that was the ultimate ground of my salvation. My movement away from this perspective and toward Calvinism went hand in hand with my growing appreciation for the whole counsel of God. I remember Dr. Van Til, professor of Apologetics at Westminster, joking that most Christians do not dare to read the first chapter of Ephesians. This chapter teaches that, before the foundation of the world, God chose those who would believe in Christ. (" . . . In love he predestined us to be adopted as his sons through Jesus Christ, in accordance with his pleasure and will—to the praise of his glorious grace, which he has freely given us in the One he loves"—Eph. 1:4-6).

At first meeting, Professor Van Til's remarks about predestination did not faze me, because I knew that I was clever enough to explain away such anti-Arminian teachings. I had done it many times! The thought soon crossed my mind, however, that such a practice was dishonest and hypocritical. Why should it be dangerous simply to let the word of God speak forth its whole glorious message?

In Mendelssohn's oratorio *Elijah* a mighty challenge sounds forth: "Bring forth your forest gods and mountain deities, and the God who by fire shall answer, let Him be God!" The first part of this solo is flung out as an awesome challenge in stentorian tones. But when the singer comes to the last words — "let Him be God!" — they are sung with such awe, reverence and fear that the singer's voice is reduced to a whisper. In these hushed tones the question penetrates: What if we have not let him be God?

The apostle Paul, in the ninth chapter of Romans, was setting forth the same doctrine when, for the sake of clarity, he raised a common objection to the doctrine of God's sovereignty. If God orders all things, why does he still blame us? How does Paul reply to this objection? Does he do it by becoming an Arminian who says that God does not really order and control all things? That might appear to man to be the best solution. But Paul, writing under the inspiration of God's Spirit, responds quite differently: "But who are you, O man, to talk back to God? 'Shall what is formed say to him who formed it, "Why did you make me like this?" ' " (Rom. 9:20). The conclusion is clear: we must let God be God!

I have read numerous articles and books stating that a commitment to Calvinism and the doctrine of the sovereignty of God will undoubtedly produce a dour, myopic, despondent view of life. For me, it was far different. For the first time I began to know true happiness in my inner spirit. I had always had a tendency toward pessimism, but when I became acquainted with the God of the Bible and came under the shadow of his wings, I became an optimist.

When we let him be God a wonderful sense of relief comes upon the believer. What is the alternative if we refuse to acknowledge this truth? If God is not sovereign over all, then he is not God. The result is no God at all! We may settle for something less than the sovereignty of God; but if we do, it means that we must look at the world as if there were no God. It is the belief in the sovereign Lord God that takes fear and uncertainty out of life. Otherwise, we become victims of the ifs — "If only I had married that other man or woman . . . If only I had chosen another profession . . . If only I had made that other investment . . . " It is belief in the sovereignty of God that banishes fear and chance from life and reconciles us to our God-ordained lot.

Certain men think this kind of faith makes for acquiescence. They believe in a kind of fatalism: since everything is predetermined, we don't have to put forth any effort at all.

This is completely false. It does not take much reflection to realize that both God's purpose and our freedom operate equally in life. It is true that there is a divinity that shapes our lives, rough-hew them though we may. For example, a man might be forced to spend one night in a strange town and then decide to make that town his permanent home; or a man might open a book, be invited to a church, or hear a particular sermon that will forever change the direction of his life. Again, he might inadvertently miss a plane or bus, and by so doing have his life spared. In all of these events it is very evident that a will other than his own is at work.

Yet man is not a mere pawn on a chessboard. Man must strive mightily to enter the straight gate; as an image-bearer of God he is both challenged by, and called to give an account to, God. Man's responsibility is clearly taught in Scripture and never negated by the teaching that God decrees whatever comes to pass.

Let us squarely face what Scripture teaches. Man is not a puppet. He does not act by someone pulling strings. He is not an automaton. The Bible is totally opposed to fatalism. Man has a will and the opportunity to choose what he will do. If he tries to excuse himself by saying it was all predetermined and therefore he had no choice, his own conscience testifies against him that he is responsible for his actions.

Of the many profitable and pleasant experiences I had at Westminster, perhaps the greatest was meeting and becoming acquainted with Dr. Machen. The name *Machen* was at one time so maligned by the modernists and semiliberal leaders of the church that I suppose I expected to see a veritable devil of a man — narrow, bigoted, somewhat decrepit, a monastic type who never smiled. To my surprise I met a fine Christian gentleman with a pleasant, almost cherubic, countenance; an overgrown boy of a man, full of fun — although his sense of humor was far above the commercial type. At the same time, he was sensitive to the needs of others and had a deep understanding of the foibles of humanity.

I cannot here relate all that Dr. Machen came to mean to me as a student and, later, as a minister of the gospel. Suffice it to say that I am most thankful that in the providence of God this man stood at the place he did at the crossroads of my life.

Machen always taught with a kind of crystal clarity so that the attentive student would often think, "Why didn't I see that before?" This was especially true of the way he explained how the biblical doctrine of predestination was the chief and only enemy of the philosophy of fatalism.

Dr. Machen explained that the plans or eternal decrees of God are not the product of blind chance, which is the case in pagan philosophy. Instead, these decrees are linked to the moral attributes of a personal God whose goodness, justice, mercy, love and compassion are boundless.

Furthermore, the same Bible that teaches predestination and election also teaches that man is a free agent. Sometimes these same two truths, seemingly so contradictory, are taught in the same verse or sentence of Scripture (see Acts 2:22, 23 and John 6:37-40). Thus, although man's free agency and God's election are difficult to reconcile in our finite minds, they are surely not irreconcilable in the divine mind.

Finally, the doctrine of predestination is most powerfully revealed to be the enemy of fatalism in the experience of spiritual conversion. When a person believes in Jesus Christ as his savior, the Bible tells us plainly that he did so because God had chosen him even before the world began. Yet, explained Dr. Machen, the act of putting our trust in Jesus is the most free decision we have ever performed. This is a simple yet profound and wonderful truth! When man fulfills the divine decree, his freedom is not taken away but rather is most fully expressed.

It is easy to fall into error on the doctrine of God's sovereignty. Both the divine election and the sincere invitation to all men to come to faith in Christ are taught in Scripture. Man falls into error when he tries to affirm one truth at the expense of the other.

Attempts to reconcile these truths typically lead to one of three responses. The hyper-Calvinist says, "I'll adopt the notion of the sovereign election of God, but I reject the part about the free agency of man." The Arminian, on the other hand, says, "I will accept the idea of man's free will, but I reject the part about the sovereign election of God." In contrast to both of these approaches the Reformed Christian says, "Since both predestination and man's free agency are clearly taught in the word of God, they must both be true. Any other view detracts from the fullness of God's revelation and the absolute extent of God's power."

As I began to understand the doctrine of the sovereignty of God, I was overwhelmed by the largeness of the gospel. The implications were astounding and the consequences transforming. To be confronted with the incomprehensible God—the absolutely sovereign God, whose every attribute is without measure — is to discover for the first time the true meaning of worship. In the presence of neither the god of liberalism nor the god of fundamentalism is the soul of man so bowed down and at the same time stretched apart. But the realization that God is sovereign expands and lifts the soul beyond human limits. Without this exalted view of God, true worship is impossible and the backbone of evangelism is removed.

I have often wondered at the smallness of the concept of God in modern-day Christianity, even in churches that call themselves evangelical. From the way they talk, you would think God is the most limited, the most hedged-about, the palest and altogether the most unnecessary of beings. He is ever and always dependent on man's choices and evidently is even quite surprised when anyone is saved.

Given this general attitude, it is not surprising that man's understanding of the love and goodness of God, demonstrated for us at Calvary, has been distorted. For when some of God's attributes are dismissed or made light of, man is led not to repentance but to indifference or presumption. By downplaying sin and its consequences, man loses the very thing for which he seeks: the assurance of God's goodness and love.

It was this heritage of a full-orbed gospel that was being lost by embracing dispensational fundamentalism. Fortunately, it was retained in the teaching at Westminster Seminary.

Westminster was important, however, not only for preserving the fullness of the Reformed faith in contrast to dispensational fundamentalism, but also for its scholarly defense of the gospel in opposition to liberalism and skepticism. Dr. Machen himself had written a number of scholarly works in defense of historic Christianity. But the central figure at Westminster regarding the defense of the faith was Dr. Cornelius Van Til.

In his method of apologetics, Dr. Van Til applied the largeness of the perspective of Reformed Christianity to the philosophical and epistemological questions of our day. For Van Til the Christian faith, based as it is on the word of God, was the only acceptable framework for reasoning correctly about the world. Thus, Van Til's system of apologetics restated the doctrine of the sovereignty of God as it relates to the entire scope of human thought.

Van Til taught that Christians must begin to develop a philosophy of God and the world based upon the triune God of the Scriptures. One cannot begin with the idea that man is the measure of truth or on some neutral ground (such as the principles of reason) and argue his way back to God. Such an approach begins by denying the very thing it seeks to affirm. If Christians are to be true to God's revelation, they must begin by accepting the Bible's description of who God is and who man is in relation to him.

According to the Scriptures, God is the self-existent, omnipotent and omniscient Creator. He knows all things fully — nothing can be added to or subtracted from God's knowledge. In the classroom, Van Til would depict the fullness of God's understanding by drawing a large circle on the blackboard:

Man, on the other hand, is not self-existent or self-sufficient like God. He is a created and finite being. However, the Bible teaches that God created man in his own image, and this makes man distinct from the other creatures in the world. In particular, man alone can think and reason after the pattern of God and in a way analogous to him. Van Til would further diagram it this way:

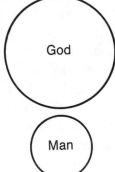

According to Van Til, man reasons properly only when he patterns his understanding of the world after God's understanding as revealed in the Bible, or as he "thinks God's thoughts after him." That is why any attempt at developing a Christian philosophy by beginning with man or the principles of reason instead of with God is ultimately self-defeating. Once man excludes God from the picture he is already guilty of faulty reasoning, for no fact in the universe can be fully and rightly understood except as that fact is related to God. To attempt to understand the world and ourselves without reference to God is the foundation of all apostate thinking. Thus we find also in Van Til a relentless application of the biblical doctrine of sin in the area of thought itself. Here is another voice crying in the wilderness, "Repent!" — this time to the fields of philosophy and science.

Van Til insisted that man can properly know and understand God, the world and himself only in the light of the divine revelation given in the Bible. Van Til's critics characterized his apologetics as an "impossible position" because it was premised on "circular reasoning." Instead, it is the only possible position.

While attending university I majored in philosophy and even did some coaching. I came to seminary thinking that I really knew something — a most dangerous assumption! I remember well how I sat up late at night with my books on logic and philosophy, building an overwhelming argument against the "impossible position" advanced by Dr. Van Til. I am glad now that I went to all that trouble. Ever since those days I have had some sympathy for, and perhaps also some understanding of, those who in late years have come to break a lance at what they call the Westminster Apologetic.

This comprehensive application of God's word to philosophy and apologetics proved effective for dealing with many thorny philosophical problems, as well as combating the philosophical underpinnings of much of liberalism. At the risk of oversimplification, let me try to explain how.

For centuries great minds have pondered the question: How can we know what is real? "Why, that's simple," one might answer. "Just look at something, just feel the object. It's real enough." But philosophers have not been satisfied with that response. They have wanted to know what is really out there after everything that is dependent upon our senses (such as taste, color and size) has been subtracted. In other words, how can we relate the *appearance* of things to the things *in themselves?*

The influential German philosopher, Immanuel Kant, wrestled with this problem and concluded that we cannot know a *Ding an sich* (thing in itself). According to Kant, the extent of our knowledge is limited to our sense experience as it is classified by the categories of the mind. Because of this, one's knowledge is restricted to what Kant called the phenomenal realm or the realm of man's experience and sense perception. One cannot know a thing in itself or discern directly the realities which may underlie or go beyond his own sense experience. These belong to what Kant termed the noumenal realm, the content of which is beyond man's ability to comprehend. Van Til would diagram Kant's position in this way:

Noumenal                 (beyond our ability to know)

▬▬▬▬▬▬▬▬▬▬▬▬

Phenomenal           (source of all our knowledge)

Kant's approach to the problem led to two implications important to theological thought. First, it made all knowledge subjective (dependent upon the knower). Second, it declared that substantial knowledge of God was impossible since such knowledge was part of the noumenal realm. Man does not have the necessary faculties to penetrate into matters above or underlying our sense experience. Struggle though he may, he is still confined to the phenomenal realm. As a result he is unsure about what he may know about God and uncertain of ultimate truth.

Post-Kantian theologians reinterpret Christianity according to this philosophical framework. Liberalism maintains that, since all knowledge is subjective, man cannot speak of the Bible as being objectively the word of God. At the same time, since Scripture speaks of subjects that are noumenal in character, man can have no certainty of the truth of its assertions. All one can do is try to live according to the code of ethics set forth in the Bible, for the validity of Scripture's doctrinal pronouncements are beyond man's ability to evaluate. This is, of course, quite different from the Bible's own declaration that it *is* the inspired and infallible word of God and man's only rule for faith and practice!

I went to Westminster Seminary having walked this dry philosophical riverbed. My university training in science and philosophy was always attempting to elbow God out of his universe. But how does one deal with the difficult problems posed by Kant and liberalism?

I recall wrestling with this question during my early weeks at Westminster. One time I was sitting in apologetics class. Dr. Van Til had drawn Kant's two-layer diagram on the chalkboard, showing the phenomenal separated from the noumenal. I was already familiar with this diagram from my previous philosophical training. Remembering that no system of thought had ever successfully crossed that great divide, I asked cautiously if it was possible for Christianity to give some answer to this insoluble dualism. Professor Van Til first responded by drawing a circle around both the phenomenal and the noumenal. Then he replied, "God created both and is revealed in both. The so-called noumenal and phenomenal are both under God and they are one in his creation and revelation. The distinction is a false one." The professor said a few more words about the Christian doctrine of creation and then continued with his lecture. But I heard no more. ["Methinks I stood amid the solemn hush of nature newly born, and there was life and there was love multiplied."] Once again I was overwhelmed with the largeness of the Reformed faith, this time as applied to the difficult philosophical and theological issues of our day.

It is significant that the largeness of the Reformed faith re-emerged at this critical time in the history of the church. It flourished in the midst of a strident, and apparently victorious, liberalism in church and state on the one hand, and remained afloat in the tidal wave of dispensational fundamentalism on the other. How essential that it continue! Let me illustrate.

When I was a boy my father had a ranch on the prairies of Alberta, Canada. In the fall of one year the normal season of drought arrived. The resulting dry and hard soil made plowing extremely difficult. All the plowshares and points quickly dulled and had to be sharpened. We were miles away from the town blacksmith; but Father, being a resourceful man, proceeded to be his own smithy. I remember how we helped the hired men cut wood and start a big fire. The steel points and shares were then put into the fire, but the steel would not get red hot. So we piled on more and more wood. The fire leaped, roared and smoked, but still the iron did not get hot enough to pound out and sharpen. We repeated the process of adding more wood. We got more smoke and more noise, but the desired golden red never appeared on those plowshares. That evening's work was quite a disappointment for the men. "A wood fire can't do it," they said.

The next morning, bright and early, I started for town with my father to see the blacksmith. The blacksmith thrust the cold steel under some coals and turned the handle of the forge with his left hand. The flames, red and blue, enveloped the iron for a few minutes. Then, with his tongs, he removed the share, now whitish red, and put it on the anvil. His heavy hammer came down expertly and the blunt cutting edge was hammered thin. While still hot, it was dipped in water and the blue crept up the iron as the proper temper was achieved. The fields could be plowed again!

That experience illustrates the necessity of the Reformed faith in these perplexing times. The fires of religion and evangelism are burning today, some think very hopefully and strong. But let us not be deceived. There may be much noise and no doubt some real heat also, but at best this is only a wood fire. It may do a lot, but it cannot do the one thing needed. It cannot give to all of life that proper temper. This requires the application of the whole counsel of God found only in the Reformed faith.

Some will say that I have spoken too harshly of fundamentalism, and I will allow that much more could be said by way of praise for some institutions than I have given. Even their sometimes-firm opposition to the Reformed faith does not lessen my appreciation for much that the fundamentalists and Bible institutes are doing. Christians may disagree, and those disagreements may generate great suffering, but the fact remains that we are still Christian brothers. Would that I had both the power and the persuasiveness to show today's fundamentalists that Calvinism, Westminster Theological Seminary and The Orthodox Presbyterian Church are among their best friends. If only the fires of Calvinism would be rekindled in the evangelical forces of America. General evangelicalism is not enough. Turn us again, oh God!

# 5

## A HOUSE DIVIDED

When Abraham Lincoln was running for the Senate against Stephen Douglas, before the War Between the States had started or was even expected to occur, he delivered his famous "House Divided" speech. Borrowing from the language of Jesus (cf Mark 3:25), Lincoln maintained that, just as a house divided against itself cannot stand, so also the United States of America could not exist half-slave and half-free.

After Lincoln composed this speech, he read it to Mr. Herndon, his law partner. Of one particular paragraph Herndon said, "It is true, but is it wise or politic to say so?" Lincoln replied, "The proposition is true and has been true for six thousand years . . . I would rather be defeated with this expression in my speech, and uphold and discuss it before the people, than be victorious without it."

The speech was roundly condemned by all who heard it. With a political campaign on, nothing could have been more unfortunate. The strong language about a house divided against itself seemed wholly inappropriate — the wrong thing at the wrong time. But in the light of subsequent history and the still-brighter light of moral law, it was an utterance that elevated Lincoln far above mere politics or even statesmanship. It was prophetic. Replying to his critics, Lincoln said, "The time has come when these sentiments should be uttered; and if it is decreed that I should go down because of this speech, then let me go down linked to the truth . . . " (cf Herndon's *Lincoln,* pp. 321-324).

The outcome of the subsequent civil strife is well known. The cost in men and matériel was staggering, but the slave was set free, the Union was saved, and Lincoln's convictions were upheld. Lincoln had counted the cost and courageously stood up for what he believed in, regardless of the possible consequences.

This same kind of courage and conviction was displayed in a different struggle involving the men in and around the "Westminster Movement." This group, in which Dr. Machen was so able a leader, held that the Presbyterian Church in the United States of America could not exist only half-loyal to the word of God. To state it more broadly, Christendom could not endure on a foundation consisting of the true gospel mixed with "another gospel." As a result of its stand, the Westminster Movement was singled out for destruction in a theological battle waged between those committed to historic Christianity and the liberal faction with its modern denials. At the heart of the debate was whether Jesus Christ was merely a good man who set a good example, or whether he was the son of God and our supernatural redeemer.

Dr. Machen, and those who stood with him, did not believe that spiritual conflicts, or even strategic battles, could be won by retreating. With the sword of the Lord in hand they marched boldly into every fray for the defense of the faith that was once for all delivered to the saints. They gave no quarter and they expected none. They opposed error and stood for the truth without hesitation or reservation. They displayed their true colors and fought openly and without subterfuge. The same was not always true of their opponents.

Dr. Mark Matthews of Seattle often expressed the wish that the modernist conspiracy could be identified as a single body so that it might be destroyed by a single blow. He was quick to point out that the tactics of the liberals were not even honest. Instead of accepting the fundamental doctrines of the church, the liberals sought to destroy those doctrines, and to replace them with liberal concepts. But the manner in which they sought to bring about change was dishonest, perhaps even diabolical. The liberals did not openly declare to the church, "Your confession is very bad, it is hopelessly outdated and unscientific. If you do not change that confession, then we cannot conscientiously be a part of such a church." Rather, the liberals assumed positions as ministers and leaders in the church and then sought to undermine the church from within. The liberals were so successful in this fifth-column activity that in a short time those who believed wholeheartedly in the Scriptures and the church's subordinate standards were either silenced or removed from the church.

How did the liberals accomplish their purpose? By appealing to the need for "tolerance" and by accusing those who opposed them of being "narrow-minded." By this strategy many of the conservatives were put on the defensive. They suddenly became timid when they were accused of intolerance or narrow-mindedness. All their resistance and discernment and even moral standards suddenly melted away. Their response to such accusations was often something like this: "Well, we don't agree with the liberals, but after all we are all Christians and we must be tolerant. Intolerance is a terrible sin. Let us never be guilty of it." In this manner those evils that would destroy the soul, the church and the nation were *welcomed* into the seminaries, pulpits and courts of the church. Never did the forces of error have an easier or more sweeping victory.

The liberals' appeal for tolerance was, however, short-lived. Once the opponents of historic Christianity gained the upper hand, the plea for tolerance came to a sudden and dramatic end. As soon as the proponents of the new and debilitating theology became entrenched in the church, those who stood for the old faith had to pay tribute or leave.

The first significant battle occurred in the Presbyterian Church in the United States of America (now the United Presbyterian Church) over the Auburn Affirmation. Its complete title was *An Affirmation Designed to Safeguard the Unity and Liberty of the Presbyterian Church in the U.S.A.* Because of its origin at Auburn Seminary, it came to be known as the Auburn Affirmation. It was published on January 9, 1924 and signed by over thirteen hundred of the ministers of the church. It was essentially a protest against the staunch witness of the 1923 General Assembly to the gospel and the historic Christian faith.

The 1923 General Assembly had declared a number of doctrines, known as the Five Fundamentals, to be essential to true Christianity. These were: the infallibility of the Scriptures, the deity of Christ and his virgin birth, the authenticity of his miracles, his substitutionary atonement, and his bodily resurrection.

The signers of the Auburn Affirmation protested that these doctrines were ". . . only theories that explained the facts." Then they elaborated: "Furthermore, such theories are in no way essential to Christianity; they should never be made tests for a minister's ordination. A man can be a minister in the Presbyterian Church without accepting such doctrines or theories."

The Affirmation revealed the campaign strategy of the modernists. The attack on historic Christianity was not to be an open, forthright one. It was to be a denial of the faith by feigned affirmations.

The following quotation from the Affirmation is reproduced as it appeared in the original. Notice how the affirmations were printed in bold-faced type, and the denials were printed in light-faced type. Referring to the action of the 1923 General Assembly, the Affirmation read as follows:

[It] . . . attempts to commit our church to certain theories concerning the inspiration of the Bible, and the Incarnation, the Atonement, the Resurrection, and the continuing Life and Supernatural Power of our Lord Jesus Christ. **We hold most earnestly to these great facts and doctrines; we all believe from our hearts that the writers of the Bible were inspired of God; that Jesus Christ was God manifest in the flesh; that God was in Christ, reconciling the world unto Him-**

**self, and through Him we have our redemption; that having died for our sins He rose from the dead and is our everliving Saviour; that in His earthly ministry He wrought many mighty works, and by His vicarious death and unfailing presence He is able to save to the uttermost.** Some of us regard the particular theories contained in the deliverance of the General Assembly of 1923 as satisfactory explanations of these facts and doctrines. But we are united in believing that these are not the only theories allowed by the Scriptures and our standards as explanations of these facts and doctrines of our religion, and that all who hold to these facts and doctrines, whatever theories they may employ to explain them, are worthy of all confidence and fellowship (Auburn Affirmation, sec. IV, second par.).

This document voiced the dominant, if somewhat hidden, theology of much of contemporary Christendom, including many in the Presbyterian Church in the United States of America. It gave expression to a faith that could say both *yes* and *no* to the great verities. It told the world that a new and wonderful faith had arisen whereby a man could claim to believe the facts of the Bible yet reject what he was pleased to call "the interpretation thereof."

The Affirmation implied that, while facts of the gospel are given by God in Scripture, the interpretation of those facts is determined by man. This is patently false. The fact that Jesus died on the cross, and the true meaning and significance of his death on that cross, are both taught in Scripture and are of divine origin. The fact of the cross cannot be separated from its biblical significance.

This attempt to separate biblical facts from their biblical significance has often been used by unscrupulous college professors to mislead their students. The professor begins by encouraging his class to doubt many things in the Bible and the Christian faith. Then, when some of the class members object or become distressed, he reassures them by saying, "It all depends on your interpretation. Your pastor interprets it one way, I interpret it another way." At this point there is generally a sigh of relief — all is well: it is only a matter of interpretation! What the students have failed to recognize, however, is that the professor has set forth a denial rather than an interpretation.

The Auburn Affirmation reflected another form of denial in its use of the word *theory*. The Five Fundamentals had always been upheld by those who have sought to uphold historic, orthodox Christianity. But in the Auburn Affirmation these facts became mere theories. This is indefensible from the Scriptures. For example, Peter at Pentecost appealed to the mighty works of Jesus as facts that attest to his deity: "Jesus of Nazareth was a man accredited by God to you by miracles, wonders and signs, which God did among you through him, as you yourselves know" (Acts 2:22). Was Peter talking about theories? No! Peter and all the other apostles referred to facts when they spoke of the mighty works of Jesus. These facts form the foundation for all subsequent doctrines of the Christian faith. Historic Christianity is abandoned if these facts and doctrines suddenly become "theories."

Dr. Machen understood this. That is why he was quick to expose the Affirmation and the liberalism upon which it rested for what it really was, namely, a different religion from the Christian faith. Indeed, when Dr. Machen lay dying in North Dakota, he was greatly distressed by the proposed visit of a minister who was an Affirmationist. He wondered why a minister who had such a different religion should come to see him at such a time.

Why did Dr. Machen feel that way? He himself crisply summed up the issues raised by the Auburn Affirmation in a manner typical of his incisive grasp of a difficult matter and his facility in exposing the nub of an issue:

> My profession of faith is simply that I know nothing of a Christ who is presented to us in a human book containing errors, but I know only a Christ presented in a divine book, the Bible, which is true from beginning to end. I know nothing of a Christ who possibly was and probably was not born of a virgin, but only a Christ who was truly conceived by the Holy Ghost and born of the virgin Mary. I know nothing of a Christ who possibly did and possibly did not work miracles, but know only a Christ who said to the wind and the waves with the voice of the Sovereign Maker and Ruler of all nature, "Peace, be still." I know nothing of a Christ who possibly did and possibly did not die as my substitute on the cross, but know only a Christ who took upon Himself the just punishment of my sins, and died there in my stead to make me right with the holy God. (Quoted in *The Presbyterian Guardian,* February 25, 1945.)

No wonder Dr. Machen did not want to die in the presence of this "other gospel"!

The Auburn Affirmation was more than a document. It marked a division in Protestantism. The number of ministers who signed it is surely significant, especially when it is certain that there were thousands of ministers who did not sign who were sympathetic with the Affirmation. The Auburn Affirmationists rapidly gained favor and authority in the denomination. They became missionaries, mission secretaries, moderators, theological professors, ministers and workers of every kind. There was not a single high office or place of influence that they did not occupy. Even the chairman of the commission that later brought Dr. Machen to trial and found him guilty was a signer of the Auburn Affirmation.

In the face of such mounting political opposition, the Westminster Movement, ecclesiastically speaking, went down to defeat. Dr. Machen and those who stood with him were brought to trial in the presbytery, the synod and finally in the general assembly. They were found guilty of violating their ordination vows and ordered suspended from the ministry.

It may seem strange that there should be such things as church trials in this modern day. You may wonder, "Were men actually put on trial for what they believed? Did this really happen in modern times? We thought heresy trials were a thing of the past." It is more unusual than that. Let the reader take careful note that, in this case, it was the *defenders* of the faith, not the challengers of it, who were put on trial. It was those who believed the great creeds of the church who were put out of the church, not those who rejected them. As one columnist put it, "Dr. Machen was tried for the heresy of opposing heresy!"

Thus it was that Dr. Machen and others went down linked to the truth; they died in the advocacy of that which was right and holy. After Dr. Machen's death (January 1, 1937), Pearl S. Buck, author and theological liberal, paid him this tribute in the January 20, 1937 issue of *The New Republic:*

> He was worth a hundred of his fellows who, as princes of the church, occupy easy places and play their church politics and trim their sails to every wind, who in their smug observance of the conventions of life and religion offend all honest and searching spirits. No forthright mind can live among them . . .

The defeat of the Westminster Movement had far-reaching significance for the Presbyterian Church in the United States of America, and the nation as a whole. But since these men stood for the word of God, it was a hollow and temporary victory that a certain faction in the church won against them. Just how hollow it was will be revealed in the chapters that follow.

During Bob's pastorate at Covenant Orthodox Presbyterian Church, Berkeley, California in 1938; *from left to right,* Bob Churchill, Dr. E. J. Young, Elders Sankey Oren, David L. Neilands, George Miles and David Kreiss

Store-front building used for worship in early beginnings of Covenant Orthodox Presbyterian Church in Berkeley, California

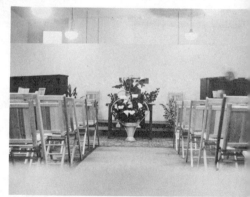

*Interior:* worship area adaptable to other activities

A new sign for Covenant Church made by one of the members tells our message

The Churchills on their 25th wedding anniversary, November 19, 1957 *Standing:* daughters Nancy and Mary with Bob and Dorothy *Seated:* Cathy (Smies) with Debbie and Norman Smies

A mission conference in June, 1958
*From left to right:* Bob Churchill, George Uomoto, Bruce Hunt, Roy Oliver, Charles Stanton, Dwight Poundstone and Robert Youmans

# 6

## A CRISIS OF MISSION

In the previous chapter I recounted how the theological division within the Presbyterian Church in the United States of America was revealed by the signing of the Auburn Affirmation. The outcome of this tendency toward liberalism was soon felt. One result, already mentioned, was the reorganization of Princeton Theological Seminary so that its faculty and board might reflect the increasingly modernist perspective of the church. Another consequence, which is the subject of this chapter, was the movement of the denominational Board of Foreign Missions away from its biblical mandate to preach the gospel, and towards modernism.

A man of letters once heard the great Irish orator, Daniel O'Connell. So impressed was he that he went home and wrote:

Once to my sight
That giant form was given,
Walled by wide air
And roofed by boundless heaven.

It was with a feeling something akin to this that I went to hear the great missionary statesman, Dr. Robert E. Speer, in the fall of 1933. Dr. Speer served as Senior Secretary of the Board of Foreign Missions of the Presbyterian Church in the United States of America.

For years the name *Speer* was a name to be reckoned with in many lands. The pastor of my church, Dr. Weyer, would often hold him up as a worthy example, both academically and spiritually. As a student in college and seminary, he outdistanced his peers. As a Christian leader and worker, he was without equal. He commanded the respect and earned the love of a great many people, both in and out of the church. The conservative forces especially acclaimed him because of his missionary vision and evangelical zeal.

The meeting at which he spoke was held in a Presbyterian Church in Media, Pennsylvania, and a large and expectant crowd had gathered. But there was decidedly more than a sense of expectancy in the air that night. Tension and the possibility of conflict were also evident.

Ever since the book *Re-Thinking Missions* with its liberal emphasis was published in 1932, the atmosphere in the denomination had been electric on the subject of missions. This book, written by an interdenominational committee on foreign missions, including two members of the Presbyterian Board of Foreign Missions, favored an eclectic religion composed of the "good" parts of all religions. According to this report, one who is a missionary "will look forward not to the destruction of these religions [of Asia], but to their continued coexistence with Christianity, each stimulating the other's growth toward the ultimate goal, unity in the completest religious truth."

Shortly after the book was published, Dr. Machen produced a pamphlet entitled "Modernism and the Board of Foreign Missions of the Presbyterian Church in the United States of America." It was written as part of a request (later denied) that the Presbytery of New Brunswick overture the general assembly to require the Presbyterian Board of Foreign Missions to uphold the historic Christian faith. The pamphlet was over one hundred pages long and recorded well-documented evidence of modernism and unbelief in the foreign missionary work of the denomination.

Dr. Machen's work was ably supplemented by a long communication from Chancellor Arie Kok, of the Dutch Legation in Peking, confirming the accuracy of Machen's charges. Here was an eyewitness account of the havoc wrought by modernism on the foreign field from one who was known and respected the world over.

Dr. Machen's pamphlet conclusively proved that the Presbyterian Church through its missions board was, to say the least, condoning modernism. His pamphlet revealed how the "new theology" and its methods, rather than merely skulking in a few church corners, had thoroughly saturated every aspect of the life and work of the denomination. As salt is in the sea, so was modernism in the church.

It was an enormously difficult task for Dr. Machen to gather his evidence of modernism in church agencies. Only a few liberal ministers and church administrators were bold enough in their viewpoints to put their non-Christian beliefs in writing. Most were either too clever or too fearful to be so open. But there was other damaging evidence readily available. It was everywhere apparent that much of the preaching, teaching and program of the Presbyterian Church was neither hot nor cold, but lukewarm. While many ministers did not actually deny such truths as the blood atonement of Christ for sin, neither did they proclaim it. Men were going to perdition under preaching that kept a discreet silence on anything offensive to the natural man. Such preaching was being heralded as a new and vibrant type of faith to meet the needs of the modern age. Thus, many sincere Christians were being called upon to sacrifice in order to push forward a faith and program that the Savior of the world would spew out of his mouth (Rev. 3:14-16).

I had not needed to read Dr. Machen's pamphlet to know of the sad state of the various boards and agencies of the Presbyterian Church. For the two years prior to that meeting with Dr. Speer in 1933 I had roomed, while attending university, at Westminster House (the name given most Presbyterian houses and student centers on university campuses in those days). Living in such an environment was an education in itself, and I am glad that I had the opportunity. I think even now of the many kindnesses shown to me by the minister's family. But the experience proved beneficial for other reasons. Westminster House was a wonderful place to meet and become acquainted with many leaders of the church, as well as to study at close range the inner life and problems of the denomination.

What I observed was both a joy and a sorrow. The pulsing life of a great university surged around me, and the church sought to respond to and meet the challenges of those strong secular currents. A few of the denominational leaders who came and spoke to the university students were sincere men of God, but more were typical modernists. The result was often frustration and confusion. I was continually confronted with the strength and awfulness of the pagan currents of the university on the one hand, and the weak and puerile message of liberalism on the other.

As a result of Machen's pamphlet, Presbyterian laymen were waking up to the fact that something was surely wrong. Among the questions they asked were: "Why were not these facts known before? . . . Why should Christians continue to support a false gospel? . . . Why doesn't our church do something?"

The church leaders themselves were on the spot. A response to the concerns of these laymen had to be forthcoming. The city of Media, Pennsylvania was chosen as the place where Dr. Speer would address these important issues. The Westminster Seminary men were there and Dr. Machen was among them. The crowd that gathered that night was filled with anticipation.

As Dr. Speer spoke, I felt certain that here was a man of God who would forthrightly address these matters. But the hour grew late and no reference was made to the burning issues that were then troubling the church. I thought to myself, "Did he not care that men were going to eternal ruin under false teaching? Why was he merely rehearsing touching events from the annals of missionary history when the enemy of souls had come in like a flood?"

For a moment I wondered if I was being too harsh. Dr. Speer began to mention modernism. There was a pause. I thought to myself, "He has saved this for the conclusion." Then he continued with the words that made such an impression on me that I believe I can still remember them exactly as they were spoken. "If there is modernism or unfaithfulness in the Board of Foreign Missions," he said, "I ought to know about it." Then, with his great hands clasped in front of him, he quoted slowly and with much feeling, John 3:16:

> For God so loved the world, that he gave his only begotten Son, that whosoever believeth in him should not perish, but have everlasting life.

The meeting was over!

I tell you I did not sleep that night. (There were to be many such nights!) How was I to think now of Dr. Speer and of the church (my church) which he had so ably served? In my student days I had greatly profited from the writings of this man. As evangelicals, I and many others felt that here was one leader in the church who was the match of any of the liberals who were denying the truths of historic Christianity. He had proved himself again and again. So how could what happened in Media be explained?

"If there is modernism or unfaithfulness in the Board of Foreign Missions, I ought to know about it," this giant of faith and intellect had said. Was there modernism in this board? None could deny it. Did Dr. Speer know about it? Who would dare say that he did not know about it? Why then did he so speak and act, on that important occasion? This was not a case of human frailty. What then was it?

Had I read further in the writings of Dr. Speer, I would have been less sure of his support for the orthodox cause. Dr. Machen had brought this point out admirably in his pamphlet. I have since concluded that Dr. Speer was a member of a large group of ministers and elders and laymen of the Presbyterian Church who, while they may have been loyal to the Scriptures in their own personal faith, had also been used to serve the cause of the Enemy because, in the midst of the conflict, they sought to remain neutral.

When I was in seminary the story was circulated that a certain professor at Princeton, while he did not himself believe in smoking, always carried matches for the boys who did smoke. Many sincere Christians tried to take the same approach in regard to modernism. As a result they became "match carriers" for liberalism, and in this way they became supporters of what was opposed to their own beliefs. To be fair, we must remember that it was very difficult to discern the deceptions of modernism. The modernist used Christian terminology, so it was not easy to detect that he was giving his terms different meanings. If we add to this the fear of many of being labeled intolerant, we can understand why many sincere Christians became willing to accommodate modernism. But the consequences were tragic.

"If there is modernism or unfaithfulness in the Board of Foreign Missions, I ought to know about it." When Dr. Speer uttered those words that night, something happened in that large audience. The tension in the air immediately began to dissipate. Many earnest Christians seemed to be saying, "What a relief to know that all this talk about doctrinal unfaithfulness in our boards is unfounded. How good it is to be a part of such a wonderful work. What a pugnacious little man this Machen must be, trying to oppose the glorious cause of the Great Commission."

The modernists were happy that night. They had triumphed in their own way, without meeting the issue squarely and without striking a blow. The cause of modernism had to be advanced, and if it could be advanced by evangelicals, or by quoting John 3:16, so much the better!

There were to be many "Medias" all over the nation as time progressed. It meant that the people in the Presbyterian Church in the United States of America were to be kept ignorant of the seriousness of modernism for a long time and with very serious results for the church. But there were those who saw the issue more clearly.

In one meeting of the Presbytery of Philadelphia a black preacher—or perhaps he was an elder—had been sitting through several meetings in which the issues of modernism in the boards and agencies of the church were being discussed. He, along with others, was informed of the unbelief, questionable procedures, and so on. Invariably, following such recitations, some very "spiritual" minister would rise and try to turn on the emotional heat. He would speak of the wonderful missionary enterprise and the constraining love of Christ, the need for brotherly love rather than criticism, and the beauty of dwelling together in unity. These monologues would usually be concluded with a quotation from the "love chapter" (1 Cor. 13).

It was by these sentiments, as well as by parliamentary sleight of hand, that the liberals at this presbytery meeting were able to keep the essential issues from being judged on their own merits. The truth or falsity of the accusations against the boards was never openly debated. Finally, this good black gentleman saw through the charade. To a group of men in the rear, he said with righteous indignation, "Gentlemen, Ah thinks the time has come when we have to live like Christ, and fight like the devil!" He was right.

It should be evident to all who look back on these events that there is no such thing as neutrality. Every Christian is called to be a soldier. Every church member is called to fight the Lord's battles. In Judges 5:23 we find a most solemn pronouncement of God against the people of Meroz: " 'Curse Meroz,' said the angel of the Lord. 'Curse its people bitterly, because they did not come to help the Lord, to help the Lord against the mighty.' " We need to take this pronouncement to heart. It is a serious thing to be one of those who, in the midst of a life-and-death struggle for the gospel, seek to be neutral and do nothing. Small wonder that the curse of the angels falls on such! Fortunately, there were others in the Presbyterian Church in the United States of America who were willing to take a stand.

# 7

## THE WORD OF MAN ABOVE THE WORD OF GOD

In the previous chapter we saw how the doctrinal defection countenanced by the Board of Foreign Missions was handled by the leaders of the church. Reform was unlikely, if not impossible. It soon became evident that candidates for service on the foreign field were being screened with bias and conservatives were not being accepted.

Students who were refused admission to the ministry or mission field because of their faith had a staunch ally in Dr. Machen. He was fond of saying that, had he remained a professor of Greek New Testament, he could have avoided involving himself in the issues by telling his students, "Sorry, boys, I'm just a professor of the Greek New Testament. I only tell you what God says in his word. I can't help what the church is doing . . ."

But instead, this "Greek professor" would often mention his concern for God's flock. "I can see through modernism," he would say. "It does not hurt my faith; but what about Christ's little ones who are being led astray?" He clearly and keenly felt a responsibility to act.

Christians in the pews also faced a dilemma. How could they in good conscience support missions financially when many of those on the field were denying the very truths that they themselves held most precious? Concerned Christians feared that, if they supported the missionaries who were allowed to teach pagans the soul-destroying doctrines of modernism, they too would be found guilty of destroying men's souls. Many tried to avoid this dilemma by designating their tithes and offerings. That is, financial gifts were sent through the regular boards but designated to certain missionaries. But this designation of funds did not hinder the modernists' program in the least. The money that was designated to pay Peter simply released that much more money to pay Judas!

It was in the midst of struggling against such difficulties that it was decided to form The Independent Board for Presbyterian Foreign Missions. Dr. Machen served as its first president. As its name and constitution clearly stated, the board was independent of any ecclesiastical control, and much debate arose about its legality.

But it was not as if such organizations had never been formed before. Similar independent agencies of a charitable, educational or literary nature had always existed in or about the church. The arguments in behalf of these groups were sound and could withstand opposition. One must also remember that it was not intended for this board to be a permanent one. It was to be dissolved when and if the official Board of Foreign Missions cleaned house.

Still, it must be admitted that it was the dictates of the heart, perhaps more than the head, that brought the Independent Board into being and caused it to address a deteriorating condition in the church. The Independent Board was not a perfect alternative. How could it be? It was not beyond criticism and questioning. But before condemning the formation of the Independent Board, one must remember the dreadful alternatives that faced the Christian in the church at that time. Consider the following facts:

- Modernism had come in like a flood, and was in control of the church.

- The word of God was not being preached in its purity.

- Candidates for mission service who took the Scriptures seriously were not being accepted since it was feared they might not work with the modernists.

- God's people were supporting that which was evil, and they could hardly disengage themselves from that coil.

- Another gospel was often preached and souls were being led astray.

Many in the church of that day were indirectly saying that if any man preach another gospel, let him be supported. Far different is Paul's message to the Galatians: " . . . If we or an angel from heaven should preach a gospel other than the one we preached to you, let him be eternally condemned!" (Gal. 1:8). How then could the church support a false gospel? That question is difficult to answer. But the fact that the church *was* supporting a false gospel is clear from two pronouncements of the general assembly delivered approximately a decade apart.

As previously mentioned, the general assembly of the Presbyterian Church in the United States of America, under conservative leadership, declared in 1923 that such doctrines as the infallibility of the Scriptures, the virgin birth of Christ, his mighty miracles, his substitutionary death, and his bodily resurrection were essential doctrines of the word of God. The Auburn Affirmation was the bold and ominous reaction to the deliverance of 1923.

In 1934 the general assembly of that same church made the following pronouncement:

> A church member or an individual church that will not give to promote the officially authorized missionary program of the Presbyterian Church is in exactly the same position with reference to the Constitution of the Church as a church member or an individual church that would refuse to take part in the celebration of the Lord's Supper . . . *(Minutes,* 1934, p. 110)

It is profitable for us to look at these two deliverances and study the changes that had taken place in the church in such a brief period. The first declaration concerned itself with the doctrines of the word of God, and declared that men should believe these doctrines because they were based on Scripture; the 1934 deliverance jumped from concern for the word of God and the purity of faith into the jangling world of church politics. In other words, the emphasis of the 1923 deliverance was on the *word of God;* the emphasis of the 1934 proclamation was on the *word of man.* A way of thinking had prevailed that no longer held God and his word in supreme and awful reverence. The church's source of authority had been shifted from God to man, and thus from truth to error.

Look again at the paragraph above taken from the assembly minutes. A church member (or church) was to support the official agencies of the Presbyterian Church. If he did not do so, it was considered to be sin, and he was in exactly the same position as if he refused to partake of the Lord's Supper. Thus support of human agencies, which may err, was put on a par with obedience to the word of God! There was to be absolutely no distinction made between Christ's command, "Do this in remembrance of me," and man's directive to "Give to support the authorized program." If one disobeyed the latter, he was just as guilty of sin as if he had disobeyed the former. The words of men and the word of God were considered equal in power and authority.

To the old-fashioned, Bible-oriented Christian, such a proposition was of course nothing short of blasphemy. The inescapable question had arisen. If official boards of the church were supporting, or teaching, denials of the word of God, how could men take vows to support such boards and be true to the Lord? How could the importance of the word of man be placed *above* the word of God?

Scripture teaches that obedience to human authority is right and proper. Christians are to be obedient to their superiors: "Everyone must submit himself to the governing authorities, for there is no authority except that which God has established. The authorities that exist have been established by God. Consequently, he who rebels against the authority is rebelling against what God has instituted, and those who do so will bring judgment on themselves" (Rom. 13:1, 2). But to place man's authority above or even on a par with God's authority is to distort scriptural teaching.

The Westminster Confession, in conformity with the word of God, condemns the absolute submission of the mind or conscience to human authority. Part of the Confession states:

> God alone is Lord of the conscience, and hath left it free from the doctrines and commandments of men, which are, in anything, contrary to His Word; or beside it, if matters of faith, or worship (ch. XX, sec. 2).

According to the Bible, the authority of the church is always subject to God's word. The church's business is to state and uphold the word of God. Its authority lies in urging obedience to God's word, not its own word. The church has authority only in the resounding words, "Thus saith the Lord." The church shines forth in fitting splendor when it refuses to impose standards that are deemed equal in importance or contrary to the word of God.

This truth, upheld by the Protestant Reformation, was lost at the 1934 General Assembly. In the name of progress, the hands of the ecclesiastical clock were turned back to a time before the Reformation or even the days of the apostles.

In the sixteenth century, the church of Rome tried to bind Luther to its own authority. But Luther held to the authority of the Scriptures and said, "Here I stand,

I can do no other!" He had a good biblical precedent for this statement. After imprisoning the apostles, the Jewish authorities commanded them not to teach or preach in Christ's name. "Peter and the other apostles replied: 'We must obey God rather than men!' " (Acts 5:29). It was this principle of authority that was violated by the pronouncement of the 1934 General Assembly.

One should bear in mind that the deliverance of the 1934 Assembly was in no way accidental or unplanned. It expressed the convictions and sentiments of a large and influential section of the church. Consequently, the idea of requiring candidates for the ministry to take a vow supporting all the agencies of the church began to take shape. Then, on September 26, 1933, the Presbytery of New Brunswick, New Jersey adopted a provision stating: "All candidates seeking licensure or ordination shall be examined as to their willingness to support the regularly authorized boards and agencies of the Presbyterian Church in the United States of America, particularly the Board of Foreign Missions."

Similarly, in a letter to the clerk of the Presbytery of Baltimore, the clerk of the general assembly wrote the following: "If and when any students from Westminster Seminary come before your Presbytery, they should be informed that the Presbytery will neither license nor ordain them until they have given written pledge that they will support the official agencies of the church, as a part of their pledge of loyalty to the government and discipline of the church" (*Minutes,* Presbytery of Baltimore, Spring, 1934).

Such requirements rapidly became the rule of procedure in other presbyteries during that time, when it was thought there might be "dangerous" men seeking ordination to the ministry or the ruling eldership. I remember one meeting of presbytery at which nine young ministerial students were asked to take that awful vow, and all nine finally agreed. They were subsequently ordained, most of them apparently without turning a hair.

Such applications of the 1934 deliverance, unpresbyterian and unbiblical as they were, became all-important. The liberals saw their advantage and were not slow in seizing it. It is chilling to recall the way they rallied around the deliverance of the 1934 Assembly and used it as an effective weapon in dispossessing Presbyterians of their rightful heritage. Ironically, these same men had cried out in "righteous" indignation against the deliverance of 1923.

While some ministerial candidates succumbed to the pressure applied to them in this fashion by the modernists, others did not. One example of this resistance was the Blackstone-Kauffroth case. These two young men, students at Westminster Seminary, applied to the Presbytery of Chester, Pennsylvania for licensure. Along with the regular examination something new was added. They were asked about their support of the denominational Board of Foreign Missions. The candidates gave the fitting answer that the board was, according to the information in hand, not entirely loyal to the constitution of the church. The presbytery subsequently did license these candidates but about one-third of that supposedly conservative presbytery voted against doing so. An appeal against the granting of licensure was even accepted by the synod although later rejected by the assembly.

This seemed to be a little cloud no bigger than a man's hand. But it was a sign of the coming storm that would break in the next two years, resulting in a division of the denomination. During that time men would be tried and suspended from the ministry of the Presbyterian Church because they would not support evil — the preaching of another gospel!

I myself was not exempt from the struggles of that time for I was due to come up for ordination soon and was anxious to know if such a vow would be required of me. I asked men from two presbyteries about this requirement. I tried to convince these men that such a vow was one that should not be taken.

It was not pleasant for me to discover how blind the men seemed to be to the evils then so prevalent in the church. Most of them thought that such a vow was nothing out of the ordinary, and the fundamentalists in my home presbytery appeared to be ignorant of, or disinterested in, such things. "Yes, Machen is right," said others, "but he is not premillennial and we cannot go along with him." When asked about the subject, one minister in Philadelphia replied, "Well, it's time you boys knew that the church has power."

One does not break with a church without experiencing some heartache and struggle. It is not easy to part from a church that has nurtured you and in which you were born anew. The most difficult issue my wife and I faced as we wrestled with our decision to leave was the question of disobeying human mandates in order to obey God. I remember after one long conversation we decided that we would stay in our denomination, at least until the constitution was changed. We decided that, since the modernists wanted the Bible-believers out, it was our duty to stay in.

Well, that night I slept well — the thing was finally settled! Or at least I thought so then. Perhaps there is some truth to the theories about the subconscious mind and how it works. At any rate, in the morning I recalled a passage I had learned years before from the Greek play *Antigone* by Sophocles. Antigone had been forbidden by the king to bury her dead brother, but she disobeyed the edict. When asked why she had disobeyed, she replied:

> Nowise from Zeus, methought, this edict came,
> Nor did I deem thine edicts of such force
> That they, a mortal's bidding, should o'erride
> Unwritten laws, eternal, in the heavens;
> Not of today or yesterday are these
> But live from everlasting.

I thought, this noble girl would make short work of the assembly's requirement! But it also troubled me a great deal that there was apparently more light in the soul of that pagan author than appeared in the Presbyterian Church.

What had happened to cause a generation of men to sell their souls so cheaply? What had happened in the Presbyterian Church that it now demanded that men take vows before almighty God to support a false gospel? The requirement to give unquestioning allegiance to human agencies was essentially the same principle by which the members of the Independent Board, including Dr. Machen, were later tried, found guilty, and suspended from the ministry of the Presbyterian Church. Others who were not on that board were also tried and found "guilty." What sin had they committed? The "sin" of criticizing the church, of telling the people the truth about modernism.

In the chapters that follow we will speak more fully of the trial of Dr. Machen and of the final triumph of modernistic policies in the Presbyterian Church in the United States of America as they relate to the formation of The Orthodox Presbyterian Church.

# 8

---

## A GENERATION ON TRIAL

In the previous chapter we learned how Dr. Machen and others felt compelled to form The Independent Board for Presbyterian Foreign Missions after all efforts had failed to prevent the sending out of foreign missionaries who did not preach the gospel. We also saw how, in the controversy surrounding the formation of the Independent Board, the 1934 General Assembly issued a statement to the effect that, if a church member did not support the official boards of the church financially, he was as guilty before God as if he refused to partake of the Lord's Supper.

On the basis of this pronouncement by the assembly, Dr. Machen and others were ordered to resign from the Independent Board, or face disciplinary action. Refusing to obey this mandate of the assembly, Dr. Machen replied: "Obedience to the order in the way demanded by the Assembly would involve support of a propaganda that is contrary to the Gospel of Christ." That statement appeared in *The Presbyterian Conflict,* by Edwin H. Rian, as well as these words: "In demanding that I shall shift my message to suit the shifting votes of an Assembly which is elected every year, the General Assembly is attacking Christian liberty; but what should never be forgotten is that to attack Christian liberty is to attack the Lordship of Jesus Christ" (pp. 16, 164).

As a consequence of his refusal, Dr. Machen was summoned to appear for a trial before the special Judicial Commission of the Presbytery of New Brunswick in February, 1935. This action was, in itself, controversial. The citation was issued in spite of the fact that Dr. Machen had transferred his membership to the Presbytery of Philadelphia the year before. On page 484 of his book, *J. Gresham Machen,* Dr. Ned B. Stonehouse explains:

> . . . Forty-four members of the Presbytery [of Philadelphia] soon filed a notice of complaint with the stated clerk of presbytery against Machen's reception, and this was later formally presented to the presbytery and carried to the Synod of Pennsylvania. It was maintained that this complaint served as a stay in the case, and that Machen's reception was not finally and officially consummated. This matter remained in a confused state for some time. Although Machen did not acknowledge the legality of the stay, he nevertheless did not refuse to deal with the Presbytery of New Brunswick when they initiated action against him in the course of the year.

This was only the beginning of many high-handed tactics displayed in the trial of Dr. Machen by the modernist-dominated New Brunswick Presbytery.

It should be mentioned here that other men were also being brought to trial at this time in different parts of the nation. One thing that characterized these "trials" was the attempt to make them secret. Church members and elders would often follow their pastors many miles to an appointed meeting place, only to find on arrival that they were locked out.

Such procedures grieved Dr. Machen deeply. He often cried out against closed and secret sessions. "What is there to hide? Open things up, and let the light of day shine in. What is there to hide from the people?" Dr. Machen's own trial was also originally to have been held behind closed doors, but he objected so strenuously that it was finally opened to the public. The trial of Dr. Machen took place in Trenton, New Jersey and lasted three days. While I do not intend to report on this important trial step by step, I do want to make clear some of its significant aspects.

Friends of Dr. Machen, and I think he himself, came to that trial with expectancy and hope. Their hopes were not for his acquittal. As nearly everyone who was aware of the liberalism in the Presbyterian Church realized, Dr. Machen's conviction was almost a foregone conclusion. No, the hope was like that of the apostle Paul—that the trial would provide an occasion to testify publicly to the gospel of Jesus Christ.

It was hoped that Dr. Machen would be able to tell the story and present evidence of modernism in the church, and to stress the need for repentance and a return to the gospel of Christ. Here, it was hoped, the evidence of unbiblical teaching in the official boards

*95*

would be laid before the court. The court would then have to deal with facts, and before the whole church it would have to give its decision. The sin of the church would finally have to be faced, and by a judicial body. The climax would be to show how the recent mandates issued at general assemblies had been contrary to the constitution of the church, and how its tenets were tantamount to putting the word of man above the word of God.

Alas, it was not to be. Dr. Machen and his defense counsel never got an opportunity to bring evidence into court in his defense. If I had my way, I would make the study of the trial of Dr. Machen in the Presbyterian Church in the United States of America a required subject in all law schools, for it became a classic example of how a man could be brought to trial and condemned without a hearing.

The mandate of the 1934 Assembly was clearly contrary to the Scriptures and the church's confession. But during the trial, any evidence from the word of God against the mandate was summarily ruled out of order. For example, the church court made the following rulings in the case of the *Presbyterian Church in the United States of America vs. J. Gresham Machen* (p. 268ff):

- This court rules that it cannot accept or hear any further arguments or references based on the Auburn Affirmation . . .

- This court rules that it cannot accept or hear any further arguments or inferences against the Board of Foreign Missions of the Presbyterian Church in the United States of America . . .

- This court rules that it cannot accept or regard any arguments questioning the legality or validity of the mandate of the General Assembly . . .

These rulings meant that certain charges were brought against Dr. Machen in court, and then he was promptly forbidden to show evidence that those charges were false and unjust.

To those with some legal background, and especially to those acquainted with the high judicial standards of presbyterianism, the most incredible ruling was the last one, which stated that the legality of the mandates of the 1934 General Assembly could not be questioned. This was a denial of an inalienable right. It was not as if a jury had listened to the facts and arguments presented, and after careful weighing of the evidence found them to be false. The ruling said with indisputable finality that no evidence of any kind that questioned the assembly's mandates could be brought into court. The court, insulated by these rulings, thus became more of an execution chamber than a court in which evidence could be considered.

There were, of course, many objections to these rulings raised during the trial. But the moderator, Dr. Culp (who, incidentally, was one of the signers of the Auburn Affirmation), always overruled these objections. I can still hear him: to each objection raised by Dr. Machen's lawyer, the gavel would come down sharply on the desk and he would say, "Objection overruled." It became an old refrain with many repetitions. The rulings, of course, allowed the prosecution to keep reiterating that there was nothing doctrinal in the case and that the church was perfectly orthodox.

But the trial also had a more maudlin, if not more sinister, aspect. On the jury that tried Dr. Machen sat the Rev. E. A. Morris, who I believe was the pastor of the host church. This man had declared both privately and publicly that, if Dr. Machen could not keep step with the overwhelming majority of the general assembly, he should get out of the Presbyterian Church. You can imagine how open-minded and impartial a man with those sentiments would be when examining and weighing the merits of the case before him! The right of a man with such convictions to sit on the jury was a prejudgment of the case and was challenged at the trial. But the modernists were in control, so this too was overruled.

During the intervals in the trial I tried to enter into some of the discussion. In all the recess-period discussions the only accusation I ever heard against Dr. Machen was that voiced by Mr. Morris — that he was out of step with the majority. That was his "unpardonable sin"! The possibility that the majority might be wrong apparently did not enter anyone's mind, nor was the abundant evidence of doctrinal unfaithfulness in the church ever considered. Rather, the general attitude was that since the majority of the church was against Machen, he had to go.

I do not think that any true American, let alone a Christian, could be in that atmosphere without feeling some fear grip his heart. Here was manifested a tyranny more sinister than that of any one man, for here was a tyranny of the majority. Yet these were the same men who had preached for years with soul-stirring conviction in praise of tolerance toward their own false views.

Since the court persisted in refusing to hear the evidence against the church boards or the decrees of the assemblies, the defense attorney for Dr. Machen summed up his case by stating that the defendant was precluded from offering the defense to which he was entitled by the constitution of the church. He further stated that he did not find himself able to present a case that would exclude those facts and arguments which had been ruled out of order.

It was, therefore, to no one's surprise that on March 29, 1935 Dr. Machen was found guilty, and ordered suspended from the ministry of the Presbyterian Church in the United States of America. It was also recommended that the sentence take effect only after an appeal to the higher courts had been heard.

There was widespread astonishment at the nature of the trial. Albert C. Dieffenbach, Unitarian editor of the column "Religion Today" in the Boston *Evening Transcript,* wrote: "It is a dramatic situation, extraordinary for its utter reversal of the usual situation in a judicial doctrinal conflict."

Dr. Daniel Russell, moderator of the Presbytery of New York, made a statement criticizing the verdict in the *New York Times* of March 31, 1935. He said, " . . . There are doctrinal differences that run into the heart of the entire problem. These the accused was not permitted to discuss in his defense."

In the June, 1935 issue of *Christianity Today,* the Rev. A. Z. Conrad, D.D., pastor of Boston's Park Street Congregational Church, described the trial as follows: "Not for a generation has anything so high-handed, so unjust, so utterly un-Christian, been witnessed as the trial of Dr. Gresham Machen in the New Brunswick Presbytery . . . "

How a jury of intelligent and professedly Christian men could conduct a court of the church in such a manner is a mystery. Perhaps there is no better explanation than that given by Professor R. B. Kuiper in the *Christian Reformed Banner,* where he wrote that the Machen trial afforded a striking revelation of the destructive influence of liberalism and liberal leanings on Christian ethics; for, said Dr. Kuiper, "It [the court] deliberately destroyed his defense beforehand."

As already mentioned, Machen was not the only one to be put on trial for his adherence to the word of God. Some of the more notable of the other trials occurred in the state of Wisconsin.

Each of the pastors I am about to mention faced this crisis of conscience and made the same decision. If a man kept silent, ease and promotion would be his portion. If he spoke up, there would be misunderstandings, enmities and possible loss of position. To the prophet Isaiah, God came on a similar occasion and spoke: "Shout it aloud, do not hold back. Raise your voice like a trumpet. Declare to my people their rebellion and to the house of Jacob their sins" (Is. 58:1).

The Rev. John J. DeWaard of the Presbyterian Church in Cedar Grove, Wisconsin was not a member of The Independent Board for Presbyterian Foreign Missions, but this fact did not prevent him and other ministers from being put on trial for speaking out against the Presbyterian Church. DeWaard brought the evidence of non-Christian teachings in the agencies of the church to a group of his church leaders. "What shall I do?" he asked them. "Shall I tell the people about it, or shall I keep quiet?" The majority said, "We'll just have to inform the people." Said a powerful minority, "No, don't tell them." Those who knew Mr. DeWaard had no question about what he would do. In his ordination vows he had promised before God and the church to speak the truth. Thus, the decision had already been made. He spoke out against the false teaching being condoned in the denomination.

As the issues and struggles unfolded in Cedar Grove, the modernists used every trick they could devise to cloud the real issue. They wanted above all else to have the people believe that there was nothing doctrinal in the affair. But the pastor and those who stood with him were more than equal to the occasion, and of course they had the advantage of having truth on their side! The presbytery told the pastor he was not to criticize the agencies of the church. In the midst of the long process of litigation, closed sessions, charges and countercharges, it was obvious that Pastor DeWaard was being tried and expelled from the church because he was telling the truth.

The resolution of the conflict came when twenty-five members of the church requested the Presbytery of Milwaukee to dissolve the pastoral relationship with Mr. DeWaard. At the same time, over three hundred members requested that the pastoral relationship not be dissolved. Nonetheless, the presbytery accepted the request of the twenty-five members opposed to DeWaard.

Finally the day arrived when Mr. DeWaard was to preach his last sermon, the 1936 Assembly having denied the appeals of the majority. During the service, a representative from the presbytery was on the platform, and at one point interfered with the service by removing the sermon notes from the pulpit. Pastor DeWaard simply walked back into the study and picked up his first draft! He then stood in the pulpit and would not move until the service was over.

People have told me with much animation what happened next. "I'll never forget it till my dying day," they would say. "The pastor gave the benediction, asked the congregation to stay and listen to the other man, and then left. And what did we do? We all got up right there in great disorder, tramping on people's toes and pushing, and left with him. We shouldn't have done it. It was rude, I guess. But you see, we had taken so much we just could not sit still any longer."

In the neighboring village of Oostburg, the Rev. Oscar Holkeboer took the same unpopular, yet courageous, stand. He, too, lifted up his voice like a trumpet, and the community heard the truth about sin in high places. When that important Assembly of 1936 made its final decision, upholding or increasing the sentences imposed by the lower church courts on the men on trial, Mr. Holkeboer not only informed his people, but told them the decisions were tantamount to placing the word of man above the word of God.

Pastor Holkeboer suffered the consequences of his stand. The *Sheboygan Press* reported the following action of the presbytery: "Be it resolved that the Milwaukee Presbytery . . . execute judgment upon the Rev. Oscar Holkeboer, such judgment being that his ordination credentials be revoked and that he be deposed from the ministry . . . " The charges that brought the judgment were "willful disregard for lawful authority . . . slander and promoting schism." In the following issue there was an excellent response from Mr. Holkeboer, revealing that he had been declared guilty of charges of slander and schism, and been sentenced, without any semblance of a trial. Besides, how could it have been "slander" to speak the truth?

In these two incidents, the great majority of the church members, both in Cedar Grove and in Oostburg, took a stand and finally left with their pastors to build new churches. I think two factors were responsible for this: the church people were well-grounded in the Reformed doctrines, and the press coverage of the issues was relatively good. I have often thought, as I review the whole situation, how different the national ecclesiastical picture might be today if in every major city there had been similar public information about the true conditions in the Presbyterian churches.

How little we realize the anguish and heartbreak, the questions, hopes and fears, of those eventful days. Some of that heartbreak was to have tragic consequences, for there was another pastor in Wisconsin who also suffered an ordeal from liberalism. I refer to the Rev. Arthur F. Perkins, of Merrill. His "great sin" was organizing a Bible conference for his young people that was free of modernist influences. He was brought to trial in Green Bay. Evidently the trial was not held behind closed doors, for the people in the north around the Menominee Indian Reservation still like to talk about that faithful pastor and that awful trial. After the trial was over, an Indian friend of Mr. Perkins said, "Preacher, you have been working on me for years. How about going to work on those preachers?"

Mr. Perkins was eventually suspended from the ministry by the Winnebago Presbytery following the fateful 1936 General Assembly in Syracuse, New York, where he and others had lost their last appeals. That is where I met him. I heard him say to his fellow condemned, "The machine never turns back; it didn't in Jesus' day." The presbytery had suspended Mr. Perkins for two years, but the assembly altered this to "suspension effective until such time as he shall repent."

Mr. Perkins arrived home in Merrill in time to hear his pulpit declared vacant by fifty-nine ministers and delegates at an executive session of the Winnebago Presbytery. He was later elected moderator of the new Wisconsin Presbytery of the Presbyterian Church of America (renamed The Orthodox Presbyterian Church after the original name was declared illegal as a result of action initiated by the Presbyterian Church in the United States of America). Indeed, the first meeting of that presbytery was held in the Perkins home.

The long strain, however, had taken its toll. No one can adequately describe the mental pain and the deep inner ache that assail a faithful shepherd of the flock when he is subjected to such actions by official governing bodies supposed to represent Christ. Shortly after the trial had ended, Mr. Perkins suffered a nervous breakdown. He went first to a clinic, then to a hospital, where he died.

The crisis exposed in these trials may have appeared to some to have arisen rather suddenly in the Presbyterian Church in the United States of America, yet in reality the situation developed slowly and over a wide geographic area. The church that tried Dr. Machen and found him guilty played only a small part in a much larger drama.

Dr. Machen, and those who stood with him, were put on trial because they resisted the currents of the age and held with heart and mind to that religion of supernatural redemption that has throughout history been known as Christianity. The doctrines and principles against which Dr. Machen fought were none other than the doctrines and principles of the age in general.

The "dear old modern mind," as Dr. Machen used to call it, was offended by the very doctrine that made Christianity the power of God in the world. This modern mind had accomplished at least two things: it had plucked out of the gospel all that offended the natural man, and it had jettisoned the whole cargo of the supernatural in Christianity as so much excess baggage.

This critical view of Christianity came to be the prevailing philosophy of the time. Not only the Presbyterian Church in the United States of America, but all the mainline American denominations, were swept into the vortex of this philosophy. Herein, I believe, lies the explanation for the abounding evil of our present day, and the accompanying indifference. Herein lies the explanation for the actions of the Auburn Affirmationists, and the doctrinal defection of the church boards and agencies.

This is the lesson that all the world should be careful to learn: When a man is liberal concerning things that are sacred and holy, he is not a true liberal in other areas of life. When a man rejects the absolute authority of God's word, he inevitably embraces other absolutes that are of an infinitely lower order. There is only *one* absolute authority that, instead of destroying human freedom, guarantees it to all men. That one supreme authority is none other than the Holy Spirit speaking to us in the Scriptures. The Bible is the *Magna Charta* of liberty. It is the holy fountain, the streams whereof make glad not only the city of God but the national life of all people as well. The importance of maintaining this charter of liberty, of keeping pure this fountain, cannot be overstated.

There is a golden cord running through every form of government constructed on scriptural principles. This cord is the recognition of a supreme authority. According to this principle, every nation and every church is to be subject to the overall authority of God speaking to us in his word. Only in this healthy atmosphere can all men be truly free in heart and conscience.

But when a nation or a church in some way or another denies this supremacy of God's revealed will, then that nation or church sets itself up as the supreme and only authority. Then, since the nation or the church usurps absolute power, it can recognize no higher authority to which appeal can be taken. Each and every citizen, therefore, is bound in an absolute way to that state, or church, since it has become all-powerful.

The mandate of the general assembly, requiring that Dr. Machen and others submit to the authority of the church itself apart from the authority of the word of God, proved painful enough to those who could not in conscience obey it. But the mandate caused larger and more-widespread evils that are not always fully comprehended. The decree also struck a blow to the vital organs of freedom itself.

Too often today, men think that there can be security and justice in the nation even if the church becomes apostate. But surely this is a precarious security. If a man is denied justice in the courts of the church, how long will justice prevail in civil affairs? The church is to be the salt of the earth and the light of the world, the spiritual teacher and example for the state. Does not history teach us that before a state is destroyed, its altars must first be polluted? It is true today, as surely as it was in ancient Israel, that "as goes the church, so goes the nation." Jesus put it thus: "For if men do these things when the tree is green, what will happen when it is dry?" (Luke 23:31).

The generation on trial in the Presbyterian Church, as represented by Dr. Machen, was one in which the fires of liberty and freedom burned with a steady, unquenchable flame. Here was unconventionality, a nonconformity that was a delight to the soul, and often lifted the drabness from life. The things that happened to Dr. Machen happened to many who bore his stamp and shared his convictions. The characteristics that he displayed were also those representative of a generation of Christians who to a large extent have now been ousted from positions of leadership in the church and nation.

In conclusion, the outcome of the trial of Dr. Machen and the others is a graphic illustration of what happens when men forsake the word of God and its expression in the grand Reformed confessions of the church. When the word of man takes the place of the word of God, the glorious world-and-life view that has been called "Calvinism" finds a prison instead of a dwelling place. It should also be said at this point that the refusal of Dr. Machen to compromise his beliefs was by no means the nonconformity of the radical, "anti-everything" type of person. No! It was deemed nonconformance by the world, but it was true to the word of God, found only where Christianity is at its purest and deepest.

The Churchills shortly after going to Sonora, California in 1961

Dedication of Calvary Church's new building
*Left to right:* Tom Champness, Henry Coray, Al Stever, Bob Churchill, Wilson Rinker

New church building for
the congregation of
Calvary Church in Sonora

The 21st General Assembly of the Orthodox Presbyterian Church meeting in May, 1954 at
Rochester, New York at which Bob served as moderator (*front row, fourth from left*)

# 9

## LAST COURT OF APPEAL

The principles of liberty found in Scripture are clearly reflected in the standards of presbyterianism. This is because they are a comprehensive summary of the teaching of the word of God. It is not in any Bill of Rights or in any human constitution, but in the Holy Scriptures, that the dignity of man and the freedom of man's conscience are adequately embodied. The essence of true presbyterianism lies not so much in presbyterianism itself, but rather in the place the word of God occupies in the life and mission of the church.

Discipline is indispensable in both civil government and church affairs. The thirteenth chapter of Romans tells us that Christians are to be subject to the higher powers, for they are ordained of God. It further teaches that rulers are not a terror to those who do good works, but to those who do evil. What an important message for our rebellious age! It is medicine both for the rulers and for the governed.

It is therefore necessary for a true church to exercise biblical discipline. If an organization such as the state or the church does not attempt to curb lawlessness, it cannot be a true representative of God on earth. That is why every Orthodox Presbyterian church member is required to vow affirmatively in response to the following question when he joins the church: "Do you agree to submit in the Lord to the government of this church and, in case you should be found delinquent in doctrine or life, to heed its discipline?"

In a Presbyterian church a man cannot be condemned for any reason other than that of disobedience to the word of God — the church may not condemn a man whom God does not condemn. The church may bind or loose on earth only that which is bound or loosed in heaven, and if it attempts to bind on earth that which is not bound in heaven, it is not administering heaven's sanctions, and the sanctions it does administer will be injurious.

All earthly authority is set up to ensure this fundamental freedom of mankind under God. When any system of government, or any court of law, violates this sacred trust, it becomes an engine of tyranny and will destroy all true freedom.

This truth is graphically symbolized in the coronation ceremony of a British sovereign. At a certain time in the ceremony, the one to be crowned is presented with an orb, representing the world. On top of the orb is a crown, signifying that all authority in this world is subject to God and Christian truth. It is a reminder that, although the rule of Britain may be worldwide and hold sway over many peoples, it must function under a higher law.

Not only governments, but also smaller groups in positions of authority, are subject to God. A tribunal of men may have its own constitution to follow, yet the exercise of its power is forever restricted by the word of God. Inherent in this understanding of the theology of the Reformation is, of course, the absolute authority of God over all other authority. This absolute authority is the wellspring of all genuine freedom among men.

It was with this belief in God's supreme authority in mind that the Reformers were careful to reiterate that all church councils may err, and have in fact erred throughout history. The corollary to this is that the motions and deliverances of church assemblies and synods are advisory and administrative. Disobedience to these decisions does not necessarily constitute sin. In fact, it may be necessary on rare occasions to disobey the mandates of councils and assemblies in order to obey the laws of God. It was against the decisions of such church councils that the apostles had to stand when they said, "We must obey God rather than men!" (Acts 5:29).

It is against the backdrop of these Reformation principles that we now return to reconsider in this chapter the final actions of the 1936 General Assembly, to which appeals from decisions of lower courts were taken by Dr. Machen and others. As we do so it will become sadly evident how the Presbyterian Church had moved away from its Reformed and biblical heritage.

The eventual outcome might have been foreseen after the actions of the previous assembly which was held in Cincinnati, Ohio in 1935. That assembly unseated three ministerial delegates who were members of The Independent Board for Presbyterian Foreign Missions. The reason given was that these men had not heeded the pronouncements of the 1934 Assembly and resigned from the Independent Board. Each delegate was given three minutes (!) to defend himself, and the moderator applied the three-minute rule assiduously, even breaking the men off in mid-sentence. Despite the fact that each of these men was a duly elected delegate in good and regular standing in his home presbytery, each one was unseated as a delegate to the assembly and denied the right to vote.

It should be noted that this move to reject the delegates was instigated by Dr. George E. Barnes, one of the signers of the Auburn Affirmation. He himself was a man who had flouted the declaration of an earlier assembly when it set forth certain fundamental doctrines of the Bible as essential. Also significant was the fact that the members of the 1935 Assembly apparently could no longer distinguish between administrative and judicial actions.

The motion of the 1934 Assembly had been purely administrative; it came from the top down, whereas all judicial acts must proceed from the bottom upward. Ministers in good standing in the Presbyterian Church were suddenly disenfranchised by an assembly without due process of law. They were denied their constitutional rights by decidedly unconstitutional acts. This was tyranny indeed! The untrained rank and file of the church was doing the bidding of an Auburn Affirmationist who had set aside the authority of the Scriptures and had put in its place the voice of the church. The church had all but ceased to be presbyterian.

It was in the wake of such actions that the all-important General Assembly of 1936 met in Syracuse. The things that I saw and heard there will live in my memory forever. I sat in the balcony, which was well-filled since many had come to witness the culmination of years of struggle in the Presbyterian Church. An increasing number of people had come to the conclusion that two fundamentally different religions were involved. The men on trial had appealed their cases to the various synods and finally to this general assembly. The cases had been handed to the Permanent Judicial Commission for review and a final decision.

The time arrived for the trial to begin. The seven members of the commission filed onto the platform while the assembly solemnly stood. The moderator announced that the assembly was about to sit in judicial capacity, and as a court of Jesus Christ. This was proper presbyterian procedure, and an important point to note, because the assembly did not consider itself to be meeting for ordinary business or administrative purposes. Thus, the decisions would not be the decisions of ordinary assemblies, as the previous ones had been. These would be the acts and decisions of the supreme court of the church and would not be altered or withdrawn unless the church repented.

The scene should have been full of dramatic tension. Although such was not the case, this very lack of tension may have indicated a drama far greater than was immediately discernible. The reason there was so little tension was that the commission did exactly what everyone expected. Three of its members were Auburn Affirmationists who had already set aside the Scriptures as the source of supreme authority and truth. That the general assembly would support the decisions of the commission was also a foregone conclusion.

Thus, the proceedings ended any hope for reform within the Presbyterian Church. In each case the decisions of the lower courts were upheld, resulting in suspension from the ministry for Dr. Machen and the others.

One might wish the devil were a brave warrior who would come out into the open and exchange blow for blow. It is often the cowardliness, the subtle underhandedness, of his attack that is so effective and so maddening. Machen and others had appealed their cases to this highest court of the church for review and decision. Surely the accused, and also the world at large, had the right to expect a rather comprehensive and incisive review of each step in the litigation.

I was expecting to hear an explanation of why Dr. Machen was tried by the Presbytery of New Brunswick instead of by the Presbytery of Philadelphia, of which he was a member. Above all, there should have been some cogent explanation as to why there could be no questioning by the accused of an assembly's mandate. Of equal importance, of course, was the fact that Dr. Machen was forbidden to bring certain materials into court as evidence that could have established his innocence. This should have had careful review and adequate reasons presented for the eventual decision. Unless the supreme court could give substantial reasons for upholding the decision of a lower court, why should appeals be made to it? I suppose that by this time we had become accustomed to this ordeal by liberalism, and did not expect too much. But when nothing was spared to give this one case all the aspects of a comic opera, it was hard to take.

A Dr. Adams came forward to announce the decision regarding Dr. Machen. Being a witty man, he brought much laughter from the assembly by ridiculing Dr. Machen. He told of Dr. Machen's supposed aspirations to a coveted chair at Princeton Seminary and suggested that Machen's subsequent attack on the church boards was caused by his frustration at not being chosen. This was completely false. Dr. Machen had indeed been offered the chair of Apologetics at Princeton Seminary, but after much consideration had written a letter declining the offer, having decided that the New Testament was his field.

Up in the balcony, two young couples were seated just in front of me. The men were either ministers or students for the ministry. As each adverse decision was given and sustained by the assembly, these men, in great excitement, would utter phrases that said in effect, "Great stuff! What a church! Imagine a church demonstrating such fearlessness, such moral strength and fortitude!" This was quite typical of the general reaction.

After that day's fateful meetings, I stood by as several liberal leaders in the fight came up to some of the ministers who had just been deposed. There was an exaggerated demonstration of good sportsmanship — the liberals smiled at the "ultrafundamentalists" and shook hands. These leaders told Dr. Machen and the other ministers that they had put up a good fight and that they respected them for it. They also told of their disgust with other fundamentalists in the church who were afraid to take similar stands for fear of losing their jobs.

Perhaps this was not a bad gesture on the part of the liberals, but it was no less tragic. Had Elijah been present, he might have cried out as he did to Ahab, "Have you not murdered a man and seized his property?" (1 Kings 21:19). The victors could afford to appear expansive and friendly — they had just secured a vast and goodly heritage. The fact that this heritage had been built through the blood, sweat and prayers of a more scripturally sound group of men meant nothing to them.

To the liberals, the church had been "rescued" from men who held the "old impossible view" that the Scriptures were the infallible and authoritative word of God.

I was glad to see at the assembly several members of the Olympia Presbytery, of which I was under care. These men came to me with interest and solicitation. They came to help me, to see that I did not leave the church. How deeply I appreciated that approach! None but a student coming up for ordination (as I expected to be doing that summer) would understand my state of mind at that time. I knew that inevitably I would have to face personally that difficult question: "In your ordination will you vow before God to support the boards and agencies of the church?"

I asked these men if such a question would be asked. "Yes," they said, "no doubt it would be." What did they think of such a question? "Well, it's probably all right." Should a minister make a blanket promise to support any human being, or agency, no matter what? "Well, perhaps not." Could a minister promise before God that he would support boards when he had in his hands evidence of the unbelief and errors that these boards were either teaching or supporting? Could a man vow to almighty God that he would support evil?

Sometimes, when ministerial candidates hesitated in answering the inevitable question about loyalty to the church boards, the questioners would rephrase it: "Don't you think you should promise to leave the church if the time came when you should find yourself in disagreement with the church?" The answer would always be yes. The modernists were always clever enough to hide their poison in a bouquet of sweet reasonableness. The question of truth was handily disposed of and the possibility of a man's contending for the faith was eliminated.

It should be made abundantly clear that a man's refusal to take such a vow is not an indication of any lack of love for the church. In fact, the very reverse is true. There is, of course, no real answer to the predicament that faced ministerial students at that time, and, I'm sorry to say, in some instances still faces candidates for the ministry in the Presbyterian Church. Thus a minister who comes into that church must become unpresbyterian at the point of entry.

The actions of this 1936 Assembly resulted, of necessity, in the formation of The Orthodox Presbyterian Church. The ministers who were found guilty were defrocked — that is, they were stripped of their ministerial credentials and no longer recognized as pastors in the Presbyterian Church in the United States of America. They did not voluntarily leave the Presbyterian Church in order to form another denomination — they were forced out and thus required to leave if they were to be able to continue preaching the gospel.

One thing at least may be said of The Orthodox Presbyterian Church. Though its numbers may be relatively small, the church stands for something quite big. No trivial matter brought about its formation. It was not a question of how much water should be used in baptism, or any of the thousand-and-one other differences between church people that have brought the various denominations and sects into being. Rather, it was an unwavering commitment to the sovereignty of God and the authority of Scripture that led to the formation of The Orthodox Presbyterian Church. Is there anything of greater importance?

The twin issues at stake in this whole struggle were the truth and the authority of God's word. Many have tried to separate these twins. They would like to believe in and preach the *truths* of the Scriptures without the sacrificing and contending that is often entailed in standing for the *authority* of the word. In like manner men would enjoy the promises, and forget the precepts.

Martin Luther faced the same two issues in his day. He had to go to the Diet of Worms even though there were "as many devils there as there were tiles on the roof tops." In believing the truths of the gospel, he found that he had to deny the authority of a decadent and corrupt church. He once said that, even though he were a small man, yet he could stand for something big in the world.

When The Orthodox Presbyterian Church was formed, it was hard for us to put the General Assembly of 1936 in proper perspective because it was so fresh in our minds. But one thing is very clear: That assembly, sitting as a court of Jesus Christ, resolutely and finally set the word of man, or the voice of the church, above the word of God. It took place in currents of secularism that were hostile, or indifferent, to Christ's overall jurisdiction. The decisions in presbyteries, synods, and finally in this highest court marked a decisive victory for a bland type of modernism invincibly ignorant of the principles upon which church and nation had been founded. Here was displayed a religious liberalism totally unable to justify itself on the intellectual or the spiritual plane. Instead, it resorted to intimidation, to the force of majorities, ridicule, misrepresentation, hush-hush policies, closed trials and even by ruling out-of-order all evidence that might be dangerous to its own position.

From that balcony in Syracuse I looked down on the proceedings of the 1936 Assembly and heard the judicial decisions. I believe I saw the death of something strong and true, something high and holy. How very much I owed to the Presbyterian Church! My wife and I had been nurtured spiritually in the church. It was all the more repugnant, therefore, to sense the odor of an evil sickness in that once healthy body.

With apologies to William Butler Yeats, I think a prophet would see in the decisions of that assembly "a shape not yet formed . . . staggering toward some Mecca to be born" (W. B. Yeats, *The Second Coming*).

# 10

## *THE WORD OF GOD ABOVE THE WORD OF MAN*

The events of the 1936 Assembly culminated the long struggle in the church between the conservatives and the modernists. The word of man was officially placed above the word of God, and men had to leave the church, or else support false doctrines. It would be hard to conceive of an issue that was more clear-cut and commanding to all honest men. In some ways the issues were larger, or more pronounced, than in Luther's day. Who, for instance, in the Roman Catholic Church at that time would have denied the virgin birth? What Roman Catholic theologian ever doubted the miracles of Christ, his penal death, or his resurrection? The modern Reformers stood for all that Luther stood for regarding the absolute authority of the Scriptures, plus a great deal more. If the situation in the sixteenth century demanded a new church, how much more the situation in the twentieth century.

So it was that, soon after this decisive 1936 Assembly in Syracuse, the "put-outers" and the "come-outers" met in downtown Philadelphia and formed a new church called The Presbyterian Church of America. The name was maintained only temporarily. Legal action against the new church taken by the Presbyterian Church in the United States of America protested the similarity of this name to its own, and forced the new denomination to select another name, which it did — The Orthodox Presbyterian Church.

One might hope that a church with such a name, and so eager to maintain the truth of the gospel against its detractors, would have a great following, but this was not so — the new church would be small, for a number of reasons.

First, the American mind-set was accustomed to religion with one eye on the box office — it judged the value of a religious movement according to the applause meter and the appeal of the movement to the masses. Sad to say, the struggle to contend for the faith was not a popular one; indeed, it was contrary to the trends of the time. For this reason many saw it as doomed from the start, and would have no part of it.

Second, there were many ministers and laymen who, while they had sympathy for the cause, were unwilling to pay the price of withdrawing from the old church. They saw clearly the drift of ecclesiastical affairs. As men were tried in presbytery and synod for their membership on the Independent Board or for speaking of the doctrinal defection in the church, it became obvious that the price of separating from the church would be considerable. It meant they would be put out of the church, lose their position, forfeit their pensions and sacrifice certain opportunities to minister and do good. This they were unwilling to do. We may not judge the motives of these men. No doubt their actions were well justified in their own minds. Still, they would not say with Luther:

Let goods and kindred go;
This mortal life also.

One of the men who remained in the Presbyterian Church in the United States of America, Dr. Clarence Edward Macartney, pastor of Arch Street Presbyterian Church of Philadelphia, came to Westminster Seminary, looking for an assistant. I was one of those he interviewed for the position. At the end of the interview he stated, "I think you may do, but there is one more question: Do you agree with this group in Philadelphia? Are you a seceder?" I was utterly surprised at the use of this term. I assured him that I was no "seceder," but that if I were asked in my ordination vows to promise before God to support modernism, I would not take such a vow. He waved this aside and later told the registrar that there was nothing "here for him."

The fact that Dr. Macartney left our ranks was a great blow, as well as a personal loss. We loved the man as a father, and had come to depend on him as a Moses or a Joshua. There were other men, of equally high caliber, such as Dr. O. T. Allis, Professor of Old Testament at Westminster, who were to stay in the Presbyterian Church in the United States of America. I like to think that such men were still with us in spirit. The cords of love and respect, though stretched, were by no means broken.

The third reason why the new church would get off to a slow start was a division that existed within the ranks of those who had come out of the Presbyterian Church in the United States of America. In the opening chapters of this book, I recounted how many churches in the Presbyterian Church, while they had struggled valiantly to preserve the truth of historic Christianity against modernism, had begun to embrace a form of doctrine contrary to that of their Reformed heritage. This was the teaching of dispensationalism. Slowly but surely, many in the church moved away from their commitment to the Westminster Confession of Faith and the larger and shorter catechisms as their statement of faith, and substituted in their place the study notes from the *Scofield Reference Bible*. This theological shift had many consequences, but one of the most serious was the way it diminished the testimony of the emerging church.

In the months preceding the fateful 1936 General Assembly an uneasiness had appeared in the ranks of those who had taken a stand against liberalism. Often I talked to ministers who were on the Independent Board or otherwise standing together in the fight against modernism. Some of these men became more and more outspoken in their assertions that they did not see eye-to-eye with Dr. Machen — meaning that he was not a dispensational premillenialist. So important was this in their eyes that they doubted if they could really stand with him in contending for the faith.

Such concerns indicated that the movement of many churches away from their presbyterian heritage towards dispensationalism was beginning to have a serious impact. To my sorrow my home church, First Presbyterian of Tacoma, became a prime example.

In 1935 (the year before Dr. Machen's trial and the events outlined in the previous chapter) I went home to Tacoma for a vacation. At the time I was still a ministerial student with one more year of seminary to complete. That morning, as I climbed the spacious stone steps of the church on Division Avenue, I was very conscious of the flow of history and of the tremendous issues at stake in the controversy that was now engulfing the denomination. I trusted that here was a church destined to take the lead in this modern warfare for the Lord. Here was a church I could unashamedly call my own!

First Presbyterian Church of Tacoma had experienced many changes in recent years. It had become a leading church in the Pacific Northwest. It had erected a fine new edifice in a most strategic location, almost doubling its original capacity. Its leadership had also changed hands, and Dr. Weyer was no longer the pastor. Soon after the new church building was erected, he had accepted a call to Duluth, Minnesota, where one night he passed away in his sleep.

Dr. Roy T. Brumbaugh was now the minister. He was a member of The Independent Board for Presbyterian Foreign Missions and was also on the Board of Westminster Seminary. It seemed that here was the man to carry forward the work and fight that Dr. Weyer had taken up. But it was not to be. While he was quicker and less ponderous than Dr. Weyer, he lacked the depth and catholicity of his predecessor. He was decidedly evangelical and fearless, yet leaned definitely to fundamentalism in the narrow sense of the word found in dispensationalism.

During Sunday School that morning I attended the men's class, taught by the pastor. Among the large number of faces in the class I noticed many young men whom I had taught and supervised in my earlier years. Now, I was glad to see, they were leaders in the church. But while I was reflecting on this my musings were interrupted by the words of the pastor, who began speaking about the fundamentalist/modernist controversy. He began saying that when the impending division comes in the Presbyterian Church, we must not make the same mistake that the earlier Reformers made when they left the church of Rome. And what was this mistake?

"Oh," said the pastor, "the error is obvious — you see, when the early Reformers left one church or denomination, they turned right around and formed another church or denomination, and this is the source of our trouble today. When this modern split comes, we must not fall into the error of forming a new denomination."

Some in the class were confused and troubled by this statement, but the majority of that large class agreed heartily with the pastor. Here was the *plus ultra* of the fight against modernism. Why hadn't people seen it before? It was "denominationalism," the organized church, that was the source of the trouble.

I was astonished. I reasoned to myself that a church leaving an older denomination would naturally have to become independent, at least for a time; but surely independentism would not prevail among people of presbyterian background. How mistaken I was! This was the effect of the dispensational teaching that for years had been making its way unhindered into the church. Dr. Brumbaugh, and many others like him, were not even in the vanguard of such teachings. They simply made a consistent application of the principles of dispensational fundamentalism.

Dr. Brumbaugh was true to his word. He and the leaders acting under his influence did not wait until the Assembly of 1936 to make the break. In August, 1935 Dr. Brumbaugh, with fifty-two elders and deacons and over five hundred members, left First Presbyterian Church of Tacoma and went across the alley where, having purchased a large Masonic building, they became The Independent Bible Church.

In my judgment, he should have waited to be defrocked or suspended along with the other ministers who had taken their stand for the word of God. Of course, it is easy to chart a man's course when you are not in the thick of the fight. But, as it was, the course of action taken by Dr. Brumbaugh and those with him diminished the opportunity to continue the ministry and uphold what had once been the precious heritage of the Presbyterian Church.

Thus it was that the changes that had been made in First Presbyterian Church of Tacoma were not merely superficial. In this quarter-of-a-million-dollar edifice, with its fine Reuter organ, its impressive gold-leaf dome and its beautiful rose windows done in real art glass — in this house dedicated to the glory of God—something tragic had occurred. Their Reformed heritage had been abandoned, and the testimony of the church of Christ was weakened and diffused.

I mention the Tacoma church because it represents the temper of much of the Presbyterian Church in its conservative sector in the period preceding the 1936 Assembly. Dr. Machen and those who marched with him against apostasy had to draw their supporters from this conservative element of the church. But many in the conservative sector had been pulled away from the breadth of true presbyterian doctrine and life into a narrow fundamentalism. We should give honor where honor is due: these people were strong in their stand against the liberalism in the older Presbyterian denomination. But their sympathy toward dispensationalism resulted in serious difficulty when The Orthodox Presbyterian Church came into existence.

These theological differences became evident at the very first general assembly of the new church. The assembly met in the New Century Club in downtown Philadelphia in early June, 1936. Dr. Machen was elected moderator, and foundation committees were appointed by the assembly. I was one of the five men who were to be examined and ordained in the first general assembly of this new church. As candidates for ordination, we had already passed several examinations given by the Credentials Committee. The final examination, on the subject of theology, was held before the entire general assembly. The assembly, not having a large docket, examined us thoroughly. After the examiner, the Rev. John Clelland, had asked us a number of questions, he turned the questioning over to the assembly.

Then it happened: someone asked us a question about the premillennial coming of Christ and the rapture of the church. This was a question related to the teachings of dispensationalism. Several ministers quickly objected, and others clamored for attention. Dr. Machen was much amused by one minister answering another minister (instead of a candidate answering a minister), and by the general confusion this created. Finally, his gavel came down firmly. "Gentlemen," he laughed, "I wish to point out the fact that the young men are not answering any of the questions." This was a wonderful way to handle a difficult situation. But while these differences provided a moment of amusement, they were soon to be a source of sorrow to the infant denomination.

Up until the time of the formation of The Orthodox Presbyterian Church, everyone had engaged in a common battle against modernism. Dr. Machen was well aware of the tides of unbelief flowing from Germany, for he had studied there; but he was not as familiar with the undertow of dispensationalism. At any rate, his awareness of modern fundamentalism never included the notion that those who upheld dispensationalism and the "pre-mil" position would weaken either the stand against liberal unbelief or the desire to maintain a truly presbyterian heritage. When this, in fact, began to take place I believe it was a surprise to him and a source of deep heartache.

As he became more aware of the danger and as the conflict increased, this time behind his own lines, he met it forthrightly, urging us to "dust off our catechism," to open our Bibles and to get our priorities in order. With the same care and precision that he had displayed in the struggles against modernism, he exposed the methods and conclusions of dispensationalism as unscriptural and dangerous. Many longed to have these clear expositions continued, but it was not to be. Dr. J. Gresham Machen died on January 1, 1937 while on a strenuous speaking tour in North Dakota.

Dr. Machen's clear stand against dispensationalism caused many conservatives to withdraw their support from The Orthodox Presbyterian Church and begin to criticize the Westminster Movement. Thus it was that, soon after the formation of The Orthodox Presbyterian Church, the new church divided again. A sizable group of churches and individuals stopped supporting West-minster Seminary and left The Orthodox Presbyterian Church to form Faith Theological Seminary and the Bible Presbyterian Synod.

While it would be wrong to say that the latter broke with The Orthodox Presbyterian Church because of a firm commitment to dispensationalism, it is true that the Bible Presbyterian Synod represented those who were more tolerant of the dispensational perspective and the "new fundamentalism." In contrast, those in The Orthodox Presbyterian Church were more concerned to maintain a commitment to historic presbyterianism and Reformed doctrine.

There was a fourth reason why the new denomination would be small: the emotionally charged question of Christian liberty. There were many in the group that first withdrew from the Presbyterian Church in the United States of America who insisted that The Orthodox Presbyterian Church needed to take a stand against such activities as movie going, card playing and the drinking of wine, to mention a few.

Dr. Machen and others in The Orthodox Presbyterian Church resisted the church's taking a stand on these matters, not because they were eager to defend the use of alcoholic beverages but because they were jealous for the word of God. How can the church of Christ add regulations and prohibitions that are not in the Bible? In particular, how can a true church defend the prohibition of activity that Jesus himself engaged in? This would be accusing the Lord himself of sin. The principial issues were of great importance. At stake was not only our Christian liberty but the integrity of the Lord and the finality and sufficiency of the word of God for Christian ethics. To maintain such high principles was costly and traumatic. The Orthodox Presbyterian Church was slandered for its stand. Public accusations of drinking in the church, such as the one that appeared in a New York paper calling The Orthodox Presbyterian Church a "wet church," were extremely difficult to tolerate and even harder to refute. We lost some fine men and churches over these matters, and you may be sure that the enemy made the most of it. Nevertheless, The Orthodox Presbyterian Church remained firm in its conviction that the word of God was to be the only rule of faith and practice.

The resistance of many to the commitment of The Orthodox Presbyterian Church to the word of God greatly reduced her testimony. Here again I must point to my own experience. Following my ordination at that first general assembly, I was sent as a home missionary to the states of Washington and Oregon. I arrived in Tacoma in 1936.

The situation in Tacoma had slowly degenerated. The new Independent Bible Church, of which Dr. Brumbaugh was pastor, had sown to the wind, and it had reaped the whirlwind. Inevitably there came a church split, then the fragments split again. Two of the splits came together again, but there were still four different groups. At one point I wrote a letter to what I considered the most promising group asking them to consider coming into The Orthodox Presbyterian Church. Back came a letter, signed by four elders, saying that they could never think of becoming part of a church that did not believe in the second coming of Christ — a totally false accusation and one which revealed how far those in Tacoma had drifted from their presbyterian and Reformed moorings.

Of the church in Seattle, I can only say that it was the same story as that of Tacoma, on a much smaller scale. I went to Seattle to minister to a large and promising group of people who were interested in becoming a new church. These people were for the most part from the church of which Dr. Mark Matthews had been pastor. There were about one hundred and fifty people, which was a very promising start indeed.

It soon turned out that neither The Orthodox Presbyterian Church, nor Westminster Seminary, met their standards of dispensational/premillenial teaching, and finally that church fell the way it was leaning. I was deeply saddened.

But time marches on, and with it go problems that had seemed insoluble. Most of the voices that were raised the loudest on these issues have already been stilled. The men who remain look back in anguish on turbulent and painful times. Though we mourn the loss, we recognize again the transience of earthly things.

The issues, too, have either changed or have in some way been modified to suit another generation. My own era is gone, but the legacy remains as a foundation for future generations. We listened, in my day, to a sound that filled us with an unholy terror. We heard the devil's laughter inside the hallowed walls of our beloved church, and were not deceived by his mockery.

Sometimes with trepidation and sometimes with less-than-perfect courage, we took our stand on the word of God and fought the devil where we stood. We placed the word of God far above and beyond the word of man — in its rightful position on the highest possible plane. We were asked to give an accounting first to God, then to ourselves and to our fellowman. And when we were queried about the rule God has given to direct us how we may glorify and enjoy him, we answered unequivocally:

> The Word of God, which is contained in the Scriptures of the Old and New Testaments, is the only rule to direct us how we may glorify and enjoy him.